Greg...
Great Lakes [barcode] ents,
I happen [barcode: D0834754]
extra copy of [...] ided
to pass it on. When this book
was written Ira North

BALANCE

A Tried & Tested
Formula For Church Growth

DR. IRA NORTH
MINISTER
Madison Church of Christ

was Senior Minister of the
biggest of the A cappella
churches of Christ — with
usually 4000 or more in
attendance. Greg, feel free
to keep this, or to pass it on
to Great Lake's Bible College
Library if and when you wish.
                    Al Meabes
            Plymouth, Michigan
            March 20, 2011

BALANCE

C O N T E N T S

INTRODUCTION

This book, *BALANCE*, will go down as one of the most far-reaching works of Ira North's life.

It is a summary of the 31 years he has spent as the regular preacher for the Madison church of Christ. It tells of the formula which he has tested, tried and proved. It is written in a very interesting style. It is readable, practical and the principles are workable. I predict a remarkable circulation for this book. It is written in his unique style and you will thoroughly enjoy it.

It is my considered judgment that brother North is the most popular and most influential preacher in the churches of Christ. A person of his ability and natural leadership appears only once in a generation. He has demonstrated the unusual ability to take a string and make it into a rope in so many ways.

For nearly 32 years, this man has worked under the supervision of great elders at the Madison congregation in Madison, Tennessee, to coordinate and help build the largest congregation among churches of Christ in all the world.

With a record Sunday school attendance that reached 8,410 in May, 1982, he stands unique among all our brethren as a builder of a local congregation. He went to Madison when there were approximately 400 members and he built a church membership of approximately 4,100 with an attendance pool—counting children under the age of accountability—of about 5,100. He will go down as "the builder of the local church" in my generation.

I have encouraged Ira North to write this book many

times. He finished the last chapters as he is in a great fight with cancer. There is material in this book which he has never published, although he has meditated upon these thoughts for years. I appreciate the comments on visitation, balance, goal setting, conducting the services, and the things that can be done by a congregation when funds are not available.

These thoughts on practical ways to bring about church growth have been written for others. These will benefit future generations of the Lord's church.

This man knows the personal benefits of church growth. He once said to me, "No church has ever loved a man more or done more for its minister than the Madison church!" Ira loves that great congregation with all his heart. No man has ever appreciated any group of the Lord's people any more than he appreciates the people at Madison.

Ira has asked me to write this introduction for what I feel will be his greatest literary undertaking. These things have been on his mind and heart for a long time. As he said, "I have reached the time of maturity and the time is now to put this in writing." Ira is "ready to go or ready to stay" as the song says. This book is a part of him that will stay with us long after he is gone.

His beloved companion, Avon, has stood by him since their senior year in high school and has been a big part of his work at Madison. She has truly been the companion of his life. They have worked as a team, and I know Avon has been a great part of his life and a major influence in the writing of this book.

Willard Collins, president
David Lipscomb College

Dedication

To my devoted wife of 44 years, and to all those who attend Sunday morning Bible school at the Madison church of Christ, this book is lovingly and affectionately dedicated.

Balance

After over 40 years in the ministry, hearing lectures on church growth, reading books, magazine articles, visiting active churches and having been the minister of a congregation that came from a little basement congregation to the largest in the world among the churches of Christ, I have come to the conclusion that there is a key word in church growth if it is solid, stable and lasting. That key word is *balance*.

In the city of Jerusalem—we have a beautiful picture of symmetry and balance.

It is impossible to overestimate the importance of balance. Balance in nature is necessary to avoid catastrophic occurrences and it is necessary for a solid, stable growth. A few years ago we visited the Yosemite Family Encampment, and while there, toured the giant redwoods of Northern California. These trees have experienced phenomenal growth. Their sheer size boggles the mind, and their height and symmetry is awe inspiring. One of the rangers explained that

9

part of the great growth of these trees may be explained by the marvelous balance in nature. He said, for example, periodically during the years lightning would start brush fires and the burning of the underbrush helped to clear the areas and make the trees grow more, nature, thus providing a balance, making possible the tremendous growth.

We see the importance of balance in the field of engineering, architecture, and mechanics. We all know what happens when a tire gets out of balance—the entire machine shakes and quakes and fails to run smooth and eventually wears out.

In the long ago there was lack of balance among the people of God. The prophet cried out, "Ephraim is a cake half baked." In the old days the art of baking a cake was pouring the batter on heated rocks. If the temperature was not right and the cake was not turned at the proper time, it could be raw as dough on one side and burnt to a crisp on the other. Ephraim was a cake half turned. He had prospered financially and physically, but had suffered spiritually.

In Luke 2:52, we have a marvelous example of a balanced growth of our blessed Lord. We are told that Jesus "grew in wisdom, in stature, and in favor with God and man." The symmetry and balance of this growth is so beautiful and wonderful that it has become the goal of Christian parents for their children and the goal of Christian education. We want our children to develop physically, socially, mentally and spiritually. It is sad when a man grows physically but fails to develop mentally. We all grieve when we see a man with a 21-year-old body, but yet the mind of a four-year-old child.

It is even sadder to see the young man that fails to grow socially. For example, a boy with a brilliant mind is started in school by his mother early and soon he is in high school. However, physically and socially he identifies with the youngsters in elementary school. He feels out of place with his peers and at every opportunity goes to those younger children for nurture. Social development is important. A man must learn to get along with all kinds of people and in all kinds of situations, and youngsters who fail to mature socially may well have some severe problems and hardships in maturity. We have all seen the consequences of a youngster pushed too fast and not given time to develop socially. He may well develop an inferiority complex, because he cannot compete in athletics and other social events because of his immaturity.

However, the saddest situation is to see a man who has developed a brilliant mind, a strong body and a good personality and yet has never developed spiritually. Intellectually he may be a giant and physically he may be as strong as one could hope, and yet if he is a spiritual dwarf, he is a cake half turned, he is a half baked individual.

In nature, in the mechanical world around us, and in individuals, it is easy to see the importance of balance.

Just as Important in Church Growth

Balance is so significant that when the New Testament tells us about the model church—the first

11

church of Christ, established A.D. 33 in the city of Jerusalem—we have a beautiful picture of symmetry and balance. The Jerusalem church was not a cake half turned. It was not a one phase congregation with one program to the neglect of all others. It had three things, yea four, that gave it a harmonious and beautiful balance. It is these things so beautifully seen in the New Testament church that we plead for in this book, and that we believe is essential to build a growing church that is not a fly by night or a splash in the pan, but will be here solid and sound year after year, decade after decade.

The church in Jerusalem had a great teaching program. They not only taught on the Lord's Day, but day to day, continuing steadfastly in the apostles' teaching. Secondly, they had a great program of evangelism and mission work. They practiced the Great Commission of going, not only across town and across the nation and across the world, but also across the street. The going church is indeed the growing church, and the mission of the church is to preach the Gospel. Thirdly, the church in Jerusalem had a great benevolent program. In fact, it took seven men full of faith and the Holy Spirit to administer this program. And lastly, it had all these things—a great teaching program, a great benevolent program, and a great mission program in the framework of the unity of the spirit and the bond of peace. This congregation, composed of thousands, was so dedicated to the unity of the spirit and the bond of peace that the scriptures say it had "one heart and one mind."

12

A Strong, Solid, Positive, Sensible Pulpit Is Essential

It pleased God through the foolishness of preaching to save them that believe, and there is no substitute for a strong pulpit in the building of the local church.

So much depends upon the pulpit. If the educational program is to be strong and vibrant, it must have encouragement from the pulpit. If members are to grow spiritually and be inspired and uplifted in their worship, they need to hear a message from the pulpit calculated to that end. A weak, or hostile, or insensitive pulpit can destroy more in a matter of minutes than can be built up with many hours of dedicated labor.

The Elevator Goes Both Ways

Remember, in talking of church growth, the elevator goes both ways. Not only is beautiful and solid growth possible, but decline is also possible. Congregations once strong become weak, and for that weakness the pulpit has to accept some responsibility.

13

Here are some case histories to illustrate this point. The case history (in some instances) may be a composite, the names having been withheld, of course, to protect the guilty.

Consider case A.

Here is a congregation located in a residential area of one of our cities in the Sun Belt. The people are middle class with good jobs and stable homes. The congregation has experienced an excellent growth, and a new building has been erected. The auditorium seats 400 and is filled to capacity. However, the congregation is not careful to see that its pulpit is filled by men who are sound in the faith, who are sensible, wholesome and positive in their approach, and the decline shortly begins. When the new preacher arrives, he arranges for one of his friends to come and hold a meeting. The visiting evangelist is essentially negative in his attitude, hostile in his disposition, and is a real "fighter." He knows how to take off the skin and rub the salt in. A remark was made to an old time preacher that the congregation was having growing pains and really making progress to which the old preacher replied, "After the Gospel Meeting, there will be no more growing pains."

Remember, in talking of church growth, the elevator goes both ways.

The prediction was prophetic, as it proved to be true. For three years the preacher continued to hammer away with his negative and hostile approach. Members were leaving slowly. As he became more radical, several were withdrawn from for failure to attend services on Wednesday night, and then the decline reached epidemic proportions. Alas, the preacher became involved with one of the deacon's wives, and along with the ineffective, radical, negative preaching, there was a scandal. This sealed the doom of the congregation, and in a matter of a few more months it was at ground zero. From an attendance of 400 to a complete wipe out in just a matter of a few short years. The building was sold and is used for a garage. It stands as a monument to what can happen to a once thriving, prosperous congregation.

Consider case B.

The congregation in case B is also located in a city in the Sun Belt. It is in one of the fastest growing sections of the state and one of the fastest growing areas in the nation. The congregation has a strong pulpit, is active and an ideal location is purchased. A beautiful building is built, the attendance is approximately 300, and the future is bright. And then, a mistake is made in employing a preacher to fill the pulpit. He has been trained in a school that places great emphasis on the negative, and it is a case where "a little learning is a dangerous thing."

His attitude is hostile and negative, and the pulpit resounds with scathing denunciations of everybody and everything. Those attending are browbeaten for those who do not attend. They leave despondent and discouraged, and the inevitable begins to happen. The members are slipping away. Week after week, month after month, the negative preacher continues. The preacher is honest and sincere. He really believes

15

the problem is that the congregation just cannot take the truth, and so he intensifies his efforts. The attendance continues to drop, until in a matter of months it is down so low that the congregation cannot pay the preacher's salary. Finally, the preacher resigns. Unfortunately, the congregation is so weak spiritually and financially that it is in danger of losing its building. A search is now on to find some congregation that will support the work long enough for the congregation to recuperate and bounce back sufficiently to be self-supporting. Their future is in doubt.

Case C.

Now, let us note another congregation in a comparable city. The congregation has 150 members and a relatively good location. The elders are fortunate in securing the service of a young man who is talented and dedicated. He is an excellent speaker and has great depth in the church. Like Barnabas, he is an exhorter and encourager. The pulpit is positive, happy, and powerful. The members leave each Sunday feeling like they have been to worship, and that they are prepared to go out and live for the Lord in the week that is ahead. The Bible school attendance begins to grow, and the worship service increases. Three years later the congregation has doubled in size. It is living in peace and harmony and has enlarged its mission budget and its work in the care of the poor. The Gospel is preached in simplicity and purity, and with the spirit of love and care and concern. The members are excited about the future, and long range plans have been made to build a new building in a better location. The pulpit should not receive all the credit, but we

16

are confident that the effective, dynamic, solid pulpit has undergirded the work and made possible the advance.

I have observed over a period of many years that congregations that grow have a strong pulpit. The pulpit may set a tone of friendliness, love, warmth, and loyalty to the Word of God, or it may set a tone that is dry, dull and uninteresting, or even browbeating, boring, and negative.

When you find a congregation with an air of excitement about its services, with members filled with joy and love for each other, you find a congregation that is anxious to share the Gospel and see others saved. When you find a congregation that has an educational program that is active and effective, take a long look at the pulpit. You will find it is preeminently positive, it is encouraging, it is strong.

There is no substitute for a strong, loyal, faithful, solid, sensible pulpit if the congregation is to grow.

Of course sin must be condemned, and the pulpit must reprove and rebuke, but it must also remember to "exhort with all longsuffering and teaching." I am convinced that one of the major differences between an effective pulpit and one that is not, is that the effective one reproves and rebukes sin, but it does not forget the exhorting with all longsuffering and teaching. It does not forget "let all things be done in love."

Many years ago I heard of a congregation looking for a preacher and two men came to visit. On the first Sunday, a man came and preached on Lazarus and the Rich Man (Luke 16). He was an educated man,

17

an excellent speaker, he had a handsome appearance in the pulpit, good English, and preached Lazarus to heaven and the rich man to hell, just as the Bible teaches. On the second Sunday, another man came. He, likewise, was handsome in appearance, educated, had a good command of the English language, and he preached the rich man in hell and Lazarus in Abraham's bosom, just as the Bible had taught.

However, the elders unanimously selected the first man to be the preacher and gave him the job. A younger member inquired of the wise old elders as to how they could arrive at such a decision. Since both men were well educated, both men were effective speakers, both men had excellent pulpit presence, both men preached the same sermon, and both men preached the truth, how could they make a unanimous decision?

"My young friend," replied one elder, "here is the reason. The second man preached Lazarus to heaven and rich man to hell. But he preached the rich man to hell with the attitude he has gone to hell, and that is good enough for him. Now, the first man taught the same truth, but when he told of the rich man being lost, it was with the attitude of oh, how tragic and sad, how heartbreaking this man could not have known the Lord and the way of righteousness, and like Lazarus have found peace and eternal bliss in Abraham's bosom."

So many times the difference between a congregation that grows and glows and one that declines and stagnates is the pulpit that preaches Lazarus to heaven, and the rich man to hell with great joy for

Lazarus and with heartbreaking sorrow for the rich man. There is no substitute for a strong pulpit that preaches the truth in love and compassion and understanding.

Away With The Funeral Home And Cemetery Atmosphere

A good atmosphere is essential in the growth of the local church.

The attitude, the spirit, the general atmosphere in a home is so important. I have visited in homes where the atmosphere is so hostile and cold that you have the feeling you could cut it with a knife. The house may be beautiful, the furniture exquisite, and the draperies and rugs very expensive, but somehow the atmosphere in the home is just not right.

The idea that the New Testament church had the atmosphere of the cemetery and the funeral home has long since been given up.

Occasionally, in the winter time we visit some friends we have at Lake Placid in Central Florida. The beautiful orange groves are a sheer delight. I am told that this section of the nation is just right in climate and atmosphere to produce this beautiful tropical fruit, and that without the climate and the atmosphere it would not be possible to produce the fruit.

The same is true spiritually. For a church to grow we must cultivate a good and scriptural atmosphere. Fortunately, this can be done in any section of the country, in any climate. It is a matter of the heart and a matter of the spirit.

From studying the New Testament, I am convinced that the churches of Christ in New Testament times were able to convey to the pagan world an atmosphere of love and care and concern that was so genuine and powerful that it melted the heart.

This same atmosphere of love and care and concern and warmth and friendliness can be cultivated and achieved today to such a degree that hearts will be melting, and outsiders will want to be a part of it.

The idea that the New Testament church had the atmosphere of the cemetery and the funeral home has long since been given up. Instead, if the book of Acts is read correctly and the tenor and tone of the New Testament, the services of the New Testament church had an atmosphere of joy. The apostle Paul teaches us to "rejoice, and again I say rejoice." Our worship services ought to be a celebration of the resurrection of Jesus, a celebration of great hope, a celebration of great love, a celebration of the providence and goodness of God.

The world is starved for friendship and love.

The growing congregation ought to be extremely anxious for everyone attending the services to feel wanted and appreciated. We, at Madison, have learned that a formal, ritualistic atmosphere does not bring growth.

Each congregation can cultivate an atmosphere of warmth and love and enthusiasm that will attract people. The Gospel of Christ is a glorious, wonderful thing. It brings such happiness to the human heart and such glorious hope to the soul.

There are ways an atmosphere that is warm and wonderful can be encouraged.

We have found the following to be helpful, particularly as the congregation grows:

1. Have an usher at every door at each service, greeting people when they come in.

2. Have a different couple assigned to every door at each service at the close to speak to all who are there.

3. We take time before each service at Madison (about 40 seconds) and ask each one to stand and shake hands with those behind them, in front of them, to their left, and to their right, to visit for just a moment before the service starts. This assures that no one present for the service feels that they are unwanted or out of place. We think it is a reverent and beautiful thing to see people speaking to each other, introducing themselves and expressing love and care.

Good Singing Is So Important

One of the greatest assets to the worship service is good singing. Dull, dry singing is so discouraging. It throws cold water on the entire worship service, and creates an atmosphere more of gloom and doom than of joy and peace. It is refreshing to attend a worship service where the song leader leads us in songs that we know with appropriate joy and enthusiasm. Song leaders can do so much in helping us have an atmosphere in the local church that is conducive to church growth.

It is hard to have an atmosphere of excitement and joy in a worship service when the singing is dead.

Attitude of Leaders

Another thing that contributes to an overall atmosphere of a balanced and growing church is the inherent philosophy of the leaders. If the leaders are negative in their outlook and fearful that the members are going to give too much, or the church is going to grow too much it will be reflected in the atmosphere. If, on the other hand, they believe in "ceiling unlimited" and hard work and growth and peace, that spirit will come through.

It is hard to deceive people in this matter of atmosphere. In my 42 years in the ministry, I have visited in many homes. Some have been very humble from the standpoint of the materialistic. Others have been lavish, and some even luxurious and ornate. However, no amount of fine furniture can hide the atmosphere and no lack of fine furniture can hide it either.

Years ago I held a meeting in Waterdale County, Alabama. I visited in the home of a couple with two little children. The little house did not have electricity or plumbing facilities. There was an outside toilet.

They brought the water in from a spring and the kitchen table had a humble oil cloth. However, this little house was as neat and clean as it could be. The meal was delicious and nutritious. And let me tell you something, there was an atmosphere in that humble little home that millions could not buy. It breathed the atmosphere of love and concern, cleanliness and wholesomeness. I enjoyed the visit; it was delightful.

I also visited a beautiful mansion on Lake Pontchartrain a few years ago. The couple who lived there were millionaires. They were very successful in business, the furniture was gorgeous and the dining room was just as nice as one you would find at the White House. The husband cooked our breakfast with his own hands, and this house, too, breathed the atmosphere of love and concern, cleanliness and wholesomeness. It was obvious that the Lord Jesus Christ and the church were the most important things in the world to this family.

Any congregation of the church on earth, whether it meets in a magnificent building costing $10 million or in a humble garage, can build an atmosphere conducive to church growth. If there is genuine love and concern, it will shine through. If there is hostility and negative feelings, it cannot be hidden with fine furniture or beautiful lighting or expensive drapes. On the other hand, if the friendliness and love are real, it cannot be dimmed with a plain and humble house.

What I am talking about here may seem subjective, and that it may be, but I can tell you it is important. I challenge you to visit a growing church with a balanced program, and without a single exception anywhere in the world you will find an atmosphere like the church of the New Testament—one of joy and excitement and of celebration and happiness.

Where There Is No Delegation There Is Stagnation

In the congregation where there is balance—a strong educational program, a strong mission program, a strong benevolent program, and all in the framework of unity of the spirit and the bond of peace—there are always leaders who know how to delegate.

It is so refreshing to see a congregation that has leaders who realize the importance of the involvement of members. An estimated 90 percent of the members at Madison are involved in some phase of the church program other than attending services of the church.

It is refreshing to see church leaders who are wise enough and good enough to delegate responsibility.

When members of the church do nothing but attend services, they tend to be proud and self-righteous. However, when they roll up their sleeves and get their

27

hands dirty in actual work for the Master, there is an absence of self-righteousness and a joy of service.

Every congregation ought to have a program of work so broad, so deep, so wonderful that every member can find a place in which he can use his talents to the glory of God and the good of mankind. The New Testament church with a strong teaching program, mission program, and benevolent program can provide involvement for every single member of the church.

This involves a leadership that knows how to delegate. I have often said that a preacher who tries to do everything himself is the world's worst preacher. Likewise, an elder or church leader who tries to do everything himself is also a poor leader.

A few years ago I visited a congregation in which one of the deacons confided in me.

"In the business world I have 5,000 people who work for me," he said. "It is an exciting, challenging job with room for growth. However, when I come to church, I am disappointed. Our elders do everything themselves, they even put in the light bulbs. We are just a group of second-hand deacons with no challenge, no program, no involvement, and nothing to do."

It is easy to understand his frustration.

Elders That Can Delegate

It is refreshing to see church leaders who are wise enough and good enough to delegate responsibility. In our program at the Madison church we have 30

28

committees. Every one of our 187 deacons serve on one or more of these committees. The elders set the policy and most of the work is done by these committees. I would like to give an example or two in order to encourage other church leaders to put your people to work and give them the latitude necessary to accomplish a task.

Example 1.

Years ago Madison became deeply involved in the care of homeless children. Our elders selected a committee of 12 headed by a dedicated doctor, who is one of our deacons. The committee selected a social worker and house parents, met regularly, and operated the program, reporting to the elders periodically and clearing all major decisions with them. By the grace of God, the cooperation of the congregation, and the unstinted labor of this committee, we have been able to take care of over 1,000 homeless children and to provide tens of thousands of hours of child care, and hundreds of thousands of dollars. If our elders had not had good sense and were not of the caliber to delegate, it would have been impossible for us to have taken care of over 1,000 homeless children. The dedicated people who serve on the committee are delighted to do the work and to give their time and talent to the project.

Example 2.

Our Mission Committee spends more money than any other committee in the congregation and as much as most all others put together. It is a time consuming responsibility to select missionaries, to visit them, to bring them in, and to keep up with them. Our Mission

Committee is composed largely of deacons and is given the responsibility (by the elders) to select the missionaries, to select the fields, and to visit them. The Mission Committee brings its recommendations to the elders, particularly on most major decisions. They are given a budget on which to operate, as well as encouragement and recognition. Members of this committee give their time to travel all over the world to visit an assigned missionary to offer encouragement and support and to keep up with their progress. If this were not delegated it just would not be done. Where there is no delegation, there is stagnation.

Example 3.

A few years ago, our people wanted a Bible kindergarten for little three and four year olds. The elders just did not have the time to organize and supervise a daily Bible kindergarten for three and four year olds so, they appointed seven members who were dedicated and trained in education and charged them with the responsibility of organizing and executing the program. The educators on this committee ran senior high schools and administered institutions all over our city. They were highly educated, well-trained, and most of all, dedicated Christians. They selected a lead teacher and a faculty and took the responsibility for the work. They have reported to the elders quarterly and kept them informed and up to date. The Bible kindergarten work has been active and has blessed the lives of little children here for a quarter of a century, yet it takes very little time and very little energy away from our elders. The reason is they know how to delegate responsibility. Where there is no delegation, there is stagnation.

In short, we recommend in every congregation in the world that the leaders learn to involve the members. Strive to develop a program that is so broad, so deep and so wonderful that every member in the church can find a place to serve in areas that they are especially talented and trained in and where they feel comfortable. This can be done when the leaders learn to delegate.

Time Is Treasure

Another positive factor in the building of the local church is respecting peoples' time. For many of us money is not our hangup nor our chief concern, but time. Time is valuable. It is so precious, in fact, that God gives it to us one moment at a time.

It is so easy to drift into a slovenliness when it comes to the services of the church.

I am convinced from many years of church work and study and observation that not only can the church have an effective worship service in one hour, but you can have a more effective, soul-stirring and heart-warming one.

The key is organization and facilitation. It is so easy to drift into a slovenliness when it comes to the services of the church. I have observed that a reputation for starting on time and getting out on time is a very valuable plus for any congregation.

33

At Madison, facilitating a service, planning it and organizing it is not a luxury but a necessity. We have duplicate worship services at 8 and 11 a.m., with duplicate Sunday Schools at 9 and 10 a.m. This means we cannot prolong a service with needless and useless announcements and comments.

Years ago the prince of preachers, N. B. Hardeman, held a meeting at Madison when he was 75 years old. One thing I noted was Brother Hardeman's attention to time. He delivered a wonderful message, but always within 30 minutes. The entire service started on time at 7:30 p.m. and was out on time at 8:30. I asked Brother Hardeman how it could be that a man 75 years old could draw such crowds night after night, and his reply I shall never forget. He said he had learned two things that most never learned in the ministry—to quit on time and to keep your mind active and alert. Brother Hardeman observed both of these points almost to perfection. He told the preachers he trained if they could not strike oil in 30 minutes, it was a dry hole and to quit boring.

I was impressed years ago when I read the story of a famous speaker who was asked how long it would take to prepare a speech of five minutes and he replied he would like to have six months. He was then asked how long he would need to prepare a twenty minute talk. He replied he would like to have a couple of weeks. And then the third question was, "how much time would you need to prepare for a one hour speech?" He replied, "I am ready to do that now."

If anyone doubts that through study and organization a person can present a powerful message in a reasonable time, read the Gettysburg Address. In the Graduate School at Louisiana State University, a candidate for the Ph.D. Degree in Public Address is sometimes asked to name the five greatest speeches in American History and justify the choice. It is always safe to name the Gettysburg Address. Dr. T. Harry Williams, the famous Lincoln scholar, made this statement one time in class. "You can know that Abraham Lincoln did not have a Ph.D. Degree, because if he had had one it would have taken him three books to have said what he did in less than five minutes in the Gettysburg Address."

However, it takes more than a skilled man in the pulpit, who knows how to organize a sermon, to keep a service on time. This of course is important, as most of us know that long sermons, for the most part, rehash and repeat information, showing a failure to organize—"the mind can only absorb what the seat can endure."

Another important thing in facilitating a service is for the song leader to lead singing instead of talking between the songs and the verses. Someone has observed that many song leaders are frustrated preachers and they just cannot announce the songs and let us enjoy singing. They have to preach a sermon between each song and tell us what the words mean as if we were children in kindergarten. When the talented Charles Nelson led singing at Madison, we had an agreement. He said, "Now, Brother North, the elders have employed you to preach to the congregation, and that is your duty, and they have asked me to lead the singing. If you will stick to preaching, I will stick to singing." It worked beautifully.

There are so many little things that can help facilitate a service. If the preacher will serve as master of ceremonies and keep everything moving, it is surprising how easy it is to have an effective worship service in one hour. You can sing five or six songs in the service, have the Lord's Supper, lay by and store, read, pray, preach, baptize ten people, and still get out on time if the service is organized.

There are several things that help facilitate the service. By having the Lord's Supper before the sermon, everyone is fresh and able to think and concentrate on the great memorial feast. By having the contribution after the sermon, it separates it from the Lord's Supper and makes possible a more effective service. Many times people are more in the mood to give after the sermon, and we have learned that if several come to be baptized you can take their confession, send them to the dressing room to get ready, and then take the Lord's Day collection. By the time the Lord's Day collection is taken, the preacher is in the baptistry ready for the baptizing. No lost motion, no waste of time, yet no sense of being in too great a hurry.

To illustrate what I am talking about, here is a case in point. Years ago an evangelist was in a meeting in a very fine small town. The graduating exercise at the high school was at 9 p.m. Therefore, he was anxious for the service to start at 7:30 and be over at 8:30 in order that people could go to the graduating service. The singer cooperated, the preacher preached for thirty minutes, and at 8:25 the invitation was extended. Twenty people came forward. Instead of taking the confession of those who came to be baptized and sending them on to prepare for the baptizing, the local preacher told first about those coming to be restored, and after lengthy remarks, had prayer. Then he took the confessions of those who came to be baptized and sent them to prepare while the audience sat in singing and in silence waiting for the baptisms.

The local preacher took more time handling the responses than it took for the entire sermon. If only he had used a little common sense he could have taken the confessions of those who had come to be baptized first, sent them to prepare, and then given the names of those who had come to be restored, had a prayer, and asked the song leader to sing one verse of an appropriate song, such as "Oh Happy Day, oh happy day, when Jesus washed my sins away," and by this time the ones to be baptized would have been ready.

What Differences Does It Make?

There are many who say, "Oh, what difference does it make? You sit three hours at a football game, why not take two hours for the worship service?" When a little mother has three children, and she gets up and gets them ready and gets them to Sunday School, leaves home at 9 a.m. and gets them to Sunday School by 9:30, and after Sunday School she goes to worship, and if she is held another two hours, she has wrestled four to five hours with those three little ones before she is home again. And then the question is: "Are we going back tonight, and are we going back for Wednesday night?" The truth is, by not respecting people's time, failing to use common sense, and failing to organize our service, we wear our people out until only a little handful come back.

You can excuse long, drawn out services and defend them all you want, but while you do it your crowds will dwindle away and your future will be impaired.

Establish A Reputation

The congregation is wise who has elders, preachers, and deacons who know the value of time. The congregation that establishes such a reputation of starting on time and getting out on time will greatly enhance its crowds. Unfortunately in so many preacher schools and so many of our Christian colleges these simple, down to earth, basic, common sense principles are never taught. I recommend if the preacher does not know how to organize and facilitate a service, that he visit some congregations that have developed the art, and see how beautiful and exciting the services are and how wonderful the attendance.

An important factor in the growth of the local church *is* a recognition of the tremendous value of time. Services *can be* organized and time can be respected without the loss of one drop of effectiveness or spirituality.

A few years ago at Madison we had a visiting preacher. We turned our pulpit over to him as a courtesy, because we wanted our people to see him and

38

know him. He took advantage of the situation and preached on and on and on. Since people who come regularly did not expect such a thing, they were worn out and disappointed. One lady stopped an elder and said, "You (the elders) have ruined my day and dinner. I thought we would have service as usual, and I set my oven with that in mind. The next time you are going to pull a stunt like this, please let us know, so at least we will not ruin our dinner and our day."

That particular preacher took advantage of a situation, but he would have been much wiser to have organized his thoughts and presented them in the time allotted. It is always better to have the audience come again and again and again rather than wear them out the first day and lose them thereafter.

Overbuilt And Underused

The church building can and should be an aid to church growth. There is no direct command to build a church building and neither is there an approved example. There is a necessary inference. The Bible teaches us to meet (Hebrews 10:25) and therefore it necessarily infers that we have a place to meet.

One of the chief hindrances to church growth, we believe, is overbuilding the auditorium.

However, the building might actually be a detriment to church growth rather than an asset. There is no substitute of course for a good location. We should be careful and not let the devil give us a lot. It is far wiser to have a good location and a less expensive building than a very expensive building on a poor location.

One of the chief hindrances to church growth, we believe, is overbuilding the auditorium. Through the

41

years we have been so prone to overbuild the auditorium and underbuild the educational facilities. Here are a couple of case studies to illustrate the point we are striving to make.

Congregation A has an active membership of 800 people. They are meeting in an auditorium that seats only 650 comfortably. They become all excited about a new building. Their zeal runs away with their judgment and they contract to build an auditorium that seats 2,300 people. Building is always exciting, and there is an air of anticipation. But, alas, the elders, the preacher, the deacons, the Bible school teachers, and the entire membership are suffering from too high expectations. The building is finished, and there is a large crowd opening day. The enthusiasm somewhat subsides as the second Sunday it is obvious they have overbuilt. There are 1500 empty seats to cool in the summer and heat in the winter. From the psychological standpoint it is devastating. Every time the preacher gets in the pulpit he has, figuratively speaking, a ton of ice water thrown on him as he gazes out into those empty pews. On Sunday night and Wednesday night it is even worse. The audience rattles around like peas in a barrel. Enthusiasm and excitement are dampened, and discouragement sets in.

It is tragic that apparently some architects and some members of the church know very little about audience reaction and the principles of effective public address. All that money and time and energy is wasted, and the budget is strained to keep up a building that is not needed. Finally, after ten long years and three changes of preachers, it dawns on the brethren what a sad mistake they have made, and they, doing the best they know how, partition off the auditorium making part of it into classrooms.

It would have been a hundred times better if that congregation had had duplicate services, utilizing the building it had, and added classrooms instead for a more effective educational program.

Consider another situation. Congregation B has a marvelous location and a growing work. They have 900 members and an auditorium that will seat approximately 900. This congregation is thinking of building an auditorium that seats 2500, and they visit us at Madison. The building committee, elders and their architect are present. We sit them down in our auditorium and make the following remarks: "Brethren, if somebody gave you a 2500-seat auditorium it would be the worst thing that could happen to you. You will have 1600 empty pews the first Sunday, and that is enough to kill any church. When we built the auditorium in which you are sitting, we had a 1,000 seat auditorium that was already filled for three duplicate services on Sunday morning. The first day we moved into this auditorium it was overflowing, and we began duplicate services the following week. But, if we had been forced to preach to empty pews and a strained budget to heat those pews in the winter and cool them in the summer it could have been an intolerable burden." My own professional training at the University of Illinois and L.S.U. in public address makes me keenly aware of how important it is to have an auditorium suitable for your purposes. If you will note on television there is never an empty seat. The curtain is dropped behind only two seats if that is all they have present. If you want to grow remember, don't overbuild your auditorium.

Underused Facilities

We have observed that congregations that really use their buildings 365 days a year, morning, noon and night, are the congregations that are growing. It is so sad to see an expensive building sitting like a museum with the exception of three hours a week. If the great corporations of America used their facilities only three hours a week, it would not be very long until they would cease to exist. In fact, some of them, like the great Dupont Company on the mighty Cumberland River in Old Hickory, Tennessee, use their plant seven days a week, 24 hours a day. Yet, in the most important work in the world sometimes our buildings are used only a few hours each week.

When you visit a million dollar building at 11 o'clock on Monday morning and it is all locked up, you know that congregation is in trouble. If finally you get in and there is one little girl with a typewriter in that magnificent million dollar building, you know there cannot be much of a program. However, if you walk in at 11 o'clock on Monday morning and it is like an insurance building with people coming and going, the halls ringing with the patter of little feet, and the classrooms echoing with "Jesus Loves Me This I Know," then you know that congregation is on the march.

Duplicate worship services also provide a wise use of the building. We have been engaged in duplicate services for 30 years, and it has saved the Madison congregation hundreds and hundreds of thousands of dollars. Someone might say, "well you really have two congregations." The answer is a thousand times no. It is the same preacher, the same sermons, the same songs, the same announcements, the same everything—it is a duplicate service. It is an expedience that is wise and affords tremendous advantages. The building is already cool in the summer and already heated in the winter, so why not use it. A business man told us one time that the multiple use of the building was the wisest thing he had ever seen a church do from a business standpoint. The Bible says "not slothful in business." We rejoice when we think of the tens of thousands of dollars that have gone to help the poor, to support missionaries on many continents, and that have gone into teaching programs, instead of in sticks and stones and brick and mortar the last 30 years. If we should decide to do away with the duplicate services, for example, in my considered judgment, it would cost us some $12,000 a week in interest on sticks and stones and brick and mortar. We need to use our buildings, not only on the Lord's day but seven days a week.

We recommend that every building be turned into a great teaching factory, and that it be used for the glory of God and the spread of the Kingdom, every hour on the hour, morning, noon and night, 365 days a year if at all possible. This book contains many suggestions of how the building can be used seven days a week, but the main thing is the policy adopted by the elders and the congregation to use the building.

If we do not have a policy of using the physical plant then it is not likely to be done. We recommend a stated policy of using the plant to the very fullest for the glory of God and the spread of the Kingdom.

Condescend To Men
Of Low Estate

It is my considered judgment that the weakest link in the program of most local congregations is in the area of benevolence. It is interesting to note that in the well-balanced, active, and dynamic program of the model church recorded in the Book of Acts, is a great benevolent program. The church in Jerusalem had such a program for the meek and the lowly, the downtrodden, and the widows, that it took seven men full of faith and the Holy Spirit to administer it. There is a great mystery in an active, wide-awake benevolent program that I cannot explain, but I have seen the results with my own eyes. It just seems that when a congregation gets involved in a program of benevolence that God opens the windows of heaven and the fountains of the deep and pours out his blessings.

A. M. Burton

The late and beloved A. M. Burton, founder and President Emeritus of the Life and Casualty Insurance

Company of Tennessee, had a profound influence on my ministry, especially so in preaching and teaching on benevolent work. Years ago he sent for me to come to his office on the 17th floor of the L & C Tower. At this time, to the best of my memory, A. M. Burton was 86 years of age and he drove every day to his office in downtown Nashville. I asked him for what purpose he had sent for me.

"I want to know how long it has been since you have preached on Romans 12:16," he replied.

"Well, Brother Burton," I said, "I don't even know what it says. What does it say?"

"It says condescend to men of low estate," he replied.

Then he asked me if I had ever gone through the Bible and recorded all the passages that taught us to help those in need. I replied that I had not, and he reached in his desk and brought out a package of papers. He told me he had gone through the Bible and copied down every passage that related to this subject and he wanted me to read them. I tried to put the papers under my arm in order to leave, but he said, "I want you to do it right now. Sit down there on that couch and read them." Well, you do not argue with a man who is 86 years old and has given his fortune to the work of the Lord. He was the only rich man I ever knew who did not pay income tax, because I understand there is a little known law that says when you give away 90% of all you make you do not have to pay income tax. Brother Burton for many years just gave it all away.

48

This grand old man called my attention to three passages of scripture.

When I had finished reading all the papers, he wanted to know when I was going to preach on condescending to men of low estate. I assured him I would do so that coming Sunday if I lived.

A. M. Burton told me that if we really practice what the Bible teaches on this subject that the church would enjoy an unprecedented growth. He said there would be countries that would build buildings and give them to us in order to have the wonderful church of Christ come over and be among them. I asked him if he had ever seen a congregation that he really thought followed the New Testament teaching on this subject to the very letter and spirit. He replied that he had known one that did during the period of its existence and the result was an average of one baptism per day and was the fastest growing and most influential church in the entire city.

This grand old man called my attention to three passages of scripture that he wanted me to bear in mind. The first was Romans 12:16, that teaches us to condescend to men of low estate. He related this interesting story.

A few years ago a rich lady in Nashville invited a few of her friends for dinner. Before the group went home she suggested they read a passage from the Bible, and asked Brother Burton if he would read the passage. Brother Burton replied that he would, of course. He opened his Bible and read Luke 14:12-13.

Since all there were multi-millionaires, it shocked them that he would read from the Holy Scriptures that when you have a dinner do not invite the rich, but instead invite the poor and those who cannot do anything for you.

The hostess was exasperated and snapped to Mr. Burton, "Why don't you and Mrs. Burton open your homes to people like that?" Mr. Burton turned to his wife and said, "Why don't we? It's what the book says." And that very week they invited twelve girls from the home on Fifth Avenue for wayward girls to come to their home for dinner. The Burtons and their children served the dinner themselves. The result of the dinner was that a Bible class was started, and ten of the twelve girls were baptized into Christ.

"What do you think would happen if every family in the local congregation opened the doors of their hearts and home to someone lonely, poor, downtrodden, and then invited them to attend the services of the church with them and hear the preacher talk about Jesus?" Mr. Burton asked.

It is easy for us to cater to the rich, to the wealthy, to the powerful, to the educated, and to the influential, but the Holy Bible commands that we condescend to men of low estate.

Another passage that A. M. Burton impressed upon my mind was Psalm 41:1-3. Mr. Burton reminded me that here are five of the greatest promises in all the Bible, and all contingent on helping the downtrodden. He also told me that in his 86 years he had lived to see the fulfillment of each one of these five great promises, and he urged me to remember that a loyal congregation in our day and time that would follow the model church in Jerusalem and have a great benevolent program would be composed of members who would also enjoy the fulfillment of these promises.

Let us note them:

1. "Blessed is he that considereth the poor: the Lord will deliver him in time of trouble."

It is easy for us to forget that there are a thousand ways an innocent man can be in serious trouble in the society in which we live. You are driving home one day, and as you turn the corner a little child dashes in front of your car, and you hit him and kill him. You do not even see the child until it is too late. It is not your fault, and you would not have done it for the wealth of the world. But a sharp lawyer who understands the system and is able to work it brings suit against you for all that you are worth plus all you can make between now and age 70. Are you in trouble? By the time you finish paying your legal fees, you will understand that an innocent man can be in serious trouble in our society.

Sometimes a man is at the wrong place at the wrong time and gets in trouble. Sometimes a case of mistaken identity can cause a man tremendous and unbelievable heartache. I remember a young man calling me one time and frantically asking for my help. He asked "Have you been reading about the sex pervert who is loose in West Nashville?" I replied yes, everyone who could read the paper had been reading about it. Then he said that a lady had just identified him as that pervert. He stated that he had not even been in that section of the city in months, and had never even thought about doing such a horrible thing. In the sensitive work in which he was in, if his picture had appeared in the paper and the charge printed, it would have done him irreparable harm. Fortunately the Chief of Police made an investigation and found it was a case of mistaken identity, and the innocent man was protected. And yet many years later, I shudder at how close that young man came to being ruined in this city and robbed of an opportunity to be a great influence for the community. Oh, there are so many ways an innocent man can be in trouble, and yet one of the great promises of Psalm 41 is the Lord will deliver him in time of trouble.

2. "The Lord will preserve him, and keep him alive."

Surely in the world that we live in today we need that providential protection. The airplanes we fly and the interstates we drive are so fraught with peril and danger. Every second of every minute of every day, we all desperately need the preserving protection of providence. If we love the poor, that divine providence is promised to us.

3. "He shall be blessed upon the earth."

The word blessed means happy, and with the time and energy and money man spends in his quest for happiness, many never understand that happiness comes as a promise fulfilled for considering the poor. Show me a congregation that is involved up to its ears in a great program for the lowly, and I will show you a congregation composed of happy people. There is no time for fussing or fighting or scratching or dividing or talking ugly about each other. There is too much to be done and there is too much joy that comes from such service.

4. "Thou wilt not deliver him unto the will of his enemies."

It is extremely difficult to contend earnestly for the faith, to have convictions on moral issues, stand for the truth and live right, and not incur enemies along the way. There is so much jealousy and envy and littleness in the world that an innocent man and a good man can accumulate enemies. Yet how wonderful to be able to turn those enemies over to the Lord. We must be interested in considering the poor, the lowly, the downtrodden, and then the Lord says in essence, "don't worry about your enemies, I will take care of that."

5. "The Lord will strengthen him upon the bed of languishing: thou wilt make all his bed in his sickness."

In everyday language this promise says "I'll take care of you when you are sick and when you are old." We think every family ought to carry hospitalization insurance, and we urge all to do so. However, in the final analysis, the best insurance in the world to be taken care of when you are old and when you are sick is the divine providence of a loving Heavenly Father. The Lord says for those who consider the poor He is going to take care of them when they are old and when they are sick.

These three great passages. Psalm 41, Luke 14:12-13, and Romans 12:16, are enough to inspire any congregation to involve their members in helping the homeless, the aged and the poor, the lowly and the downtrodden. Fortunately, in our society today, there are many programs that a local congregation can do. We have found a great and wonderful blessing in providing homes for homeless children, in providing for our elderly, and in assisting the poor. Retired men and women have so much to give, and we have been delighted to learn that many of them are willing to give their time in this kind of a program. Ladies of the congregation can sew, the clothing room can be manned by volunteers and the food room can be maintained for those in need. Even the little children in Sunday School enjoy bringing food for those who are in need.

There are people who are old and poor and unable to have one good balanced meal a day. Many congregations now have a program of "Meals on Wheels" where volunteers cook a meal each day, and others of the congregation volunteer to deliver the route. The county health nurse will furnish names of those truly in need of this kind of service. Our program of "Meals on Wheels" has been going for about 20 years. We have been privileged to provide one good balanced meal a day for many people in need. We have been so pleased over so many volunteering to give their time for such a program. Others have volunteered to provide much of the food. The program has not been an undue burden on the church treasury, but has brought good will from so many and has been such a blessing.

Several years ago our retired men asked for a place where they could rebuild furniture for the poor. Our elders provided them an aluminum building on the back of the parking lot and bought them a truck. These elderly men painted the truck to read "Madison church of Christ, Dealers in Faith, Hope and Charity." Over the last quarter of a century, they have provided furniture for many families in need, and it has been such a blessing to these men to be able to give their time in a significant work.

Evangelistically Oriented

We are convinced that the benevolent program should be evangelistically oriented. This does not mean that we should help only those we convert. The Bible says we are to do good unto all men, but especially to those of the household of faith (Galatians 6). However, there is certainly nothing wrong when you help people to invite them to Sunday School and try to get the children enrolled in a Bible class. We have converted many hundreds of people through our benevolent program. True, we have helped many hundreds and thousands who were not members of the church and were not converted, but when we assist them we tell them what they really need and what all of us need is the Lord Jesus Christ.

A few years ago I was at the church building by myself. The offices were closed and the building locked. I heard a timid knock on the door, and when I went to the back door there were two little girls about six and eight years of age. I opened the door and asked if I could be of any help. The oldest little girl said, "Mr., is this the church what helps people?" I threw up my hands and said, "Well, I will declare.

There are 750 churches in this town, and you have found the right one. This is indeed the church what helps people." And the little girl told me that their father was ill and out of work, and they were hungry. I told them this was a problem that could be solved. I took them to the food room and loaded them down with all the groceries they could carry. As we were going down the hall I said, "Girls, do you go to Sunday School?" They replied, "No sir, we don't." And then I showed them the department that was for their age and asked them if they would like to come Sunday. They replied that they surely would, and I assured them they would be welcome and that I felt like they would really enjoy the classes.

We have reached so many hundreds of people with our benevolent program. It is truly Christian love in action. Everything the local congregation does should be evangelistically oriented, for our real goal is the souls of men and women.

The Golden Key
To Church Growth

The golden key to church growth is found in Ephe-
sians 4:4. It is imperative to keep the unity of the
spirit in the bond of peace. We often forget in church
growth that the elevator can go both ways. Sometimes
it takes more prayer, effort, patience, wisdom, and
work to keep a congregation built than it does to build
one. Over and over again we have seen congregations
grow only to slip backwards. In 99 times out of 100
the explanation for the backwards slide is the failure
to keep the unity of the spirit in the bond of peace.

**The number one problem in the local congregation
today is keeping the unity of the spirit in the bond
of peace.**

Paul pleaded with the church in Philippians 2, "let
each esteem others better than themselves." I like
Phillips Translation in this particular passage in which
he says, "if Christ means anything to you at all, learn
to live together in harmony."

The number one problem in the world today is the failure to live together in harmony, and unless it is solved (to a reasonable extent) there may well be an atomic holocaust that would destroy civilization as we know it. We read with revulsion and heartache about the hatred and the bloodshed in the Middle East and we grieve over the carnage in Northern Ireland, as well as our own cities. What a shame human beings have not learned, in all these thousands of years, to live together in harmony.

The number one problem in the home today is also learning to live together in harmony. The skyrocketing divorce rates and the trail of broken homes, and orphaned children is eloquent testimony to the tragedy of a divided home. If a father and mother cannot learn to live together in harmony and keep the unity in the home, they have failed in one of the greatest adventures of life.

Finally, the number one problem in the local congregation today is keeping the unity of the spirit in the bond of peace. The late and beloved Stan Lillie, one of the greatest elders I have ever known, made this statement: "Let's face it, the number one problem, the number one challenge, and the number one job we have as elders is to keep the unity of the spirit in the bond of peace. If we fail to do this in the local congregation, we have failed as elders. Let us never lose sight of it."

The Power of Unity

We have all seen the power of unity. Remember the story that our older preachers used to tell when preaching on unity.

An old man before he died gathered his eight sons around him for a last talk before crossing Jordan. He had gathered eight hickory sticks and tied them together, and he asked each boy to test his strength by seeing if he could break the bundle of sticks. The oldest tried first and was unable to do so. Each son tried his strength through the youngest and all failed. Then he untied the bundle of sticks and gave them a stick at a time, and said, "now see if you can break it", and of course they accomplished the task easily. Then he drew the lesson of unity, "When I am gone I want you boys to remember that if you stay together you will be strong and unbreakable, but if you divide and fuss and fight among yourselves, it will be an easy matter for you to be broken."

The Bible has much to say about the matter of unity. In bygone days we have applied most of these great passages to the denominational world, and while this is applicable, every one of these passages apply to the local congregation.

The Tragedy of Division in the Local Congregation

Somehow we have never been able to get across to the average congregation the tragedy of division. In the early years of my ministry I believed that it would take 50 years to get over a first class church fuss. In my latter years, I have changed my mind. I am not sure a congregation ever really gets over a tragic fuss and split. The animosity is passed from generation to generation, and it is like the bird with the broken wing, it never soars as high again.

59

I often tell the congregation at Madison something like this: "Today we assemble in great joy and great happiness, and in an atmosphere of tremendous good will and Christian love. This congregation has never had a fuss. It has never had a split. It has never had a division. We have always preached and practiced the love of Christ and the love of each other. The beauty of this peace is so wonderful that it surpasseth understanding. God forbid that anything should ever happen to it. But if something should happen that we had a church fuss, a split or a division, the little children sitting here on the front seat would never live long enough to see what we are all experiencing today."

How precious and important is that unity of the spirit in the bond of peace. A congregation can have the greatest teaching program in the world, it can have the greatest mission program in the world, and it can have the greatest benevolent program in the world, but unless it follows the teaching of the New Testament and the example of the church in Jerusalem and puts it all in the framework of the unity of the spirit in the bond of peace, its growth will be stunted, its future uncertain, and its influence greatly diminished.

Unity Like Life is Delicate

So many things that are precious are delicate. Unity, like life, is so precious and so delicate. For example, while life is so valuable, it can be quickly snatched away and anyone reading this book could lie a corpse at the funeral home this time tomorrow. Think, too, how delicate and priceless is the unity of the spirit in the bond of peace. It should never be taken for granted or taken lightly. It will not come easy, and it will not be preserved without blood, sweat, toil and tears.

It Can Be Done

Although unity is delicate, priceless, and precious, it can be preserved. We may not be able to solve the problems of the nation and the world, but each congregation, regardless of its size, whether it is 10 or 10,000, can keep the unity of the spirit in the bond of peace. If the congregation is to hold its growth and to continue its growth, it needs to make an irrevocable, absolute commitment and dedication to the unity of the spirit in the bond of peace. We are committed to worshiping on the Lord's Day, for we believe this to be the teaching of the scriptures. We are committed to observing the Lord's Supper on the Lord's Day, for this is the teaching of the scripture (Acts 20:7). We are committed to immersion for baptism, and this is good. Now, we need to make that same commitment to the unity of the spirit in the bond of peace.

The plain truth is, 99 percent of all problems in the local congregation are not matters of doctrine, but matters of judgment and personality. We must not and should not make any compromise on matters of principle and doctrine, but we must learn to live together in harmony and do all that we do in love and with an eye to the teaching of the holy scriptures on the unity of the spirit in the bond of peace.

"As The Bible School Goes So Goes The Congregation!"

C. J. Garner has been preaching the Gospel for over 50 years. He is currently on our staff and is a great inspiration to us. He is the first minister I know to publish a church bulletin. He did so primarily to encourage attendance at the Sunday morning Bible school. C. J. was careful to mail the bulletin where each member would receive it on Friday or Saturday morning. Thus, he was able to achieve the maximum effect for attendance and interest the coming Sunday in Bible school.

Part of the balance of a loyal, faithful New Testament church is a strong educational program.

Many denominational churches have emphasized Sunday school to the neglect of the worship services. It is not unusual to find a denominational church with considerably more in attendance in Sunday school than in worship service. However, among churches of Christ the very opposite is true. It is not unusual to find a congregation whose Bible school attendance is only one half the attendance at the worship service.

One of C. J. Garner's favorite expressions is, "as the Sunday School goes, so goes the congregation." I believe he has something. I believe in the educational program of the church, and any congregation that fails to develop it is not going to achieve the balance necessary to even start to begin to reach the peak of its potential.

So much depends upon our knowledge of the Word of God. (See II Peter 3:18). We are comforted by the Word of God (Romans 15:4), we are kept by the Word of God, we are led by the Word of God (cf. Acts 20:32; I Peter 1:5; Romans 10:17), and we grow by the Word of God (I Peter 2:2). The congregation that goes all out for its educational program, encouraging every member to attend, and providing the proper incentive, motivation and training for its teachers will be the congregation that will look forward to healthy growth.

I believe in the educational program of the church, because it provides a steady, solid growth that lasts and endures. I would like to offer a few recommendations for achieving a quality educational program.

1. Provide adequate opportunity for teachers to improve themselves. I recommend the summer workshop at Abilene Christian University in Abilene, Texas. This summer lectureship is conducted each year for the purpose of better preparing Bible school teachers in teaching every age level. The program is consistently of high quality and provides a great opportunity

for teachers to improve themselves. Congregations are urged to spend some money in sending their teachers and providing them an opportunity to attend. There are also many regional workshops, where teachers share techniques and methods that can be of great help.

From our own experience, Madison has learned that providing at least one workshop each year for our teachers pays dividends in upgrading the quality of our educational program.

2. The educational program of the church should be given a high priority from the pulpit and in the church bulletin. A pulpit that is neutral on the educational program is a pulpit that discourages rather than encourages. The church bulletin that is filled with reprints of poems and articles rather than blazing with enthusiasm and encouraging the local educational program is a church bulletin that needs revision.

3. Recognition for Bible school teachers is recommended. The dedicated men and women who teach the classes are not seeking recognition and do not want it. However, they should have it chiefly so that they will be reminded and all others will be reminded of how important a contribution teachers make. Many congregations have an appreciation dinner each year in which a visiting speaker is invited, and some elder speaks expressing thanks from the entire congregation for the service that is rendered. Such an occasion is ideal to present certificates or special awards for teachers who have taught for a number of years and who have given so much for the ongoing of the pro-

gram. It is sad when some dedicated teacher gives 20 years of service and no one is thoughtful enough to publicly say thank you.

4. The church leaders should give the educational program high priority in matters of budget. It does cost something to have a classroom well equipped with adequate materials and lesson helps, charts, maps, and grafts are expensive. However, when we consider the value, the cost is really minimal. Each growing Sunday school should have an Art Department in which men and women with artistic talent can donate their time to help the classroom blaze with enthusiasm. An attractive room, well equipped with the proper furniture and adequate aids is an asset.

5. A periodic study should be made of the organization of the Bible school. The Bible says, "let all things be done decently and in order." Good organization in the Bible school adds to the quality and effectiveness of the teaching program. Many congregations have discovered gold mines of talent that could be utilized in the educational program of the church. A talent search in each congregation might well pay a great dividend.

Have A Sunday School Drive Each Year

I am a great believer in setting goals and having attendance drives in Bible school work. The goal in every Sunday school ought to be one more for Christ. I am often asked, "How many do you want in Bible school?" The answer is simply one more. The Bible teaches us to leave the 99 and go after the one. We should be willing to do anything that is legal and morally right to get one more student to come and study with us about our blessed Lord Jesus.

It is true, when we have a Bible school drive that we do not keep all the contacts we make, but the point is we keep some, and interest is increased and enthusiasm is generated. The Sunday school drive is an excellent method to smoke out lukewarm members who fail to realize the necessity of backing the educational program.

It has been the experience of many of us that the spring and the early fall are the ideal times for such a drive. The spring is a good time because winter is over, people are feeling better, and the springtime just seems ideal for a new beginning. The early fall is ideal, because school vacations are over, the children are back in school, the weather is favorable, and psychologically it seems to be an ideal time for the drive.

Super Sunday School Drive Every Five Years

A super Sunday school drive about once every five years is recommended. It has been our experience that a well-organized drive about once every five years in which you strive to set a new attendance record at the local congregation pays dividends. In our last drive our goal was for 8,002. The two were you and me. We were fortunate to reach 8,410. We used 43 billboards, television commercials, radio commercials, newspaper advertising, direct mail, personal advertising, and promotional pieces such as buttons, pencils, and balloons for children. Also, we pitched a large tent on the back of the lot in order to have a fellowship dinner. We advertised it as the "Feeding of the 8,000 in 20 minutes." We had considerably more than 8,000 and fed them in 15 minutes with 80 serving lines. It was an old fashioned basket dinner. We asked each one of our families to bring enough food for their own plus six people. With over two thousand family units this gave us enough food for approximately 12,500. The fellowship dinner provided excitement and happiness and joy and fellowship.

Another feature of our Bible school drive is the bringing in of outstanding speakers to teach classes on special subjects. This gives us an excellent excuse to invite our friends and neighbors to hear these men speak on subjects which they have done a great deal of preparation on and have proven effective.

"What about the cost?"

The cost of a super Sunday school drive is considerable. We have found through experience that the drives pay for themselves and then some. Our contribution on the day of our last drive was $6,000 above everything that we spent. Now, if a Sunday school drive is not worth one Sunday's contribution, then we ought to forget it. The truth of it is, you cannot put the value on such a thing.

We baptized five people as the result of the drive the first two days after it was over. We expect to baptize people for years to come from contacts that were made on this great and happy day.

68

What About the Criticism?

But someone says, "Yes, but what about the criticism you get when you have a Bible school drive?" Our answer to that is the good you do outweighs the criticism a hundred thousand times. Those who criticize are generally the poor souls who are born in the objective mood and the kickative case. They are always looking to criticize someone else but are woefully lacking in showing us the way to grow in the reaching of new souls for Christ. It is my considered judgment, after 30 years in the ministry at the Madison church, that congregations that are paralyzed by the fear of criticism can just throw in the towel as far as church growth is concerned. Another interesting thing is that the criticism you receive is always from those outside who are as a rule, lukewarm. The members of the congregation are thrilled to be a part of a growing, going work and are thrilled to see things being done.

Our advice to every congregation that loves the Lord and wants to reach souls, is don't let the dissenters make the decisions. Don't be afraid of criticism. We advocate a philosophy of progress and growth in every way possible that is consistent with the Word of God. The philosophy is not peace at any price, principle must be placed first, and these questions are to be asked:

(1) Is this right?

(2) Is this scriptural?

(3) Will this please the Lord Jesus?

(4) Will this advance the cause of Christ?

When these are carefully answered, the course is carefully set, and we (at Madison) go all out. We determined many years ago not to be afraid of petty criticism. We know the Bible, we know what the church is, and we know what its mission is, and when the course is clear and we know we are right, we are determined not to be stopped or even slowed by criticism. We are determined that the dissenters will not make the decisions.

The educational program of the church offers us the great and glorious opportunity for solid, permanent growth. We urge every member of the local congregation to support the educational program of the church. Give it your time, your attendance, your energy and your help in every way you can. The truth of it is that most of the additions to the congregation come from the educational program, and those that are not converted largely through the educational program of the church must be integrated into such a program or eventually we lose them.

Part of the balance of a loyal, faithful New Testament church is a strong educational program. It is worth the patience and the time and the prayer and the money and the effort to achieve it.

Building
A Team Ministry

For many years providing a team ministry was feared. The reason was simple—when you bring in more than one preacher, you are courting division. If there is jealousy or envy or competition between the preachers, and some members line up behind one and some behind another, then you are in trouble. However, I soon became converted to the tremendous value of a team ministry. As the congregation grew and the program grew, it was inevitable with so much to be done that one preacher simply could not spread himself thin enough to go around. At one time I literally served in every field of church work. I was my own educational director, youth director, associate minister, marriage counselor, visitation minister, personal evangelism minister, etc. It became apparent that the congregation could not continue to grow without some help.

Now I am sold on the tremendous value of a team ministry. I recommend that congregations add to their team as their financial strength and numerical strength warrants. However, to keep balance I have some suggestions to make.

It is essential in a team ministry that every minister be committed irrevocably to keeping the unity of the spirit in the bond of peace. There are some preachers with personalities that just simply will not fit working on a team. They must be the top dog and are unhappy in a team situation. This type of preacher makes a grave mistake when he accepts work on a team. However, there are hundreds of preachers and maybe thousands who can fit into a team situation, and not only fit in, but find that it makes their work so much more enjoyable. What a wonderful thing it is to have someone to help you when you are on vacation, or when you are sick, or when you are too busy to get around to all the countless chores, and know that the work will be done. We have observed that as the congregation grows, if it builds a good team ministry it continues to prosper. You will note that in congregations like Garland Road in Dallas; Central church in Amarillo, Texas; Overland Park in Kansas City; Centerville congregation in Centerville, Tennessee; Graymere church in Columbia, Tennessee; and Sixth and Izard in Little Rock, Arkansas; that you will find that they all have this in common—a dedicated group of preachers working together as a team to advance the cause of Christ.

Now I am sold on the tremendous value of a team ministry.

There are some who say you simply cannot have two preachers that will work together in peace and harmony and love. This simply is not the case. We have ten here on our staff, and we each have our areas of responsibility. The elders have even given us instructions in writing as to what we are expected to do. There is a clear understanding, and we can truthfully say as far as we know there is not one grain of sand in our team of ministers. We love each other, we need each other, and we appreciate each other. Here at Madison it is my privilege to serve as the preacher with the primary responsibility of the pulpit, editing the paper, and influencing the entire staff and membership to work together in peace and harmony.

Jim Mankin is our dearly beloved associate whose office is next door. He teaches a Sunday school class of 1,200 on Sunday morning, a Ladies Bible Class on Tuesday, a large adult class on Wednesday and handles the pulpit, bulletin, etc. when I am absent.

Bruce White is responsible for our marriage and family counseling service, which has offices on the ground level and assists families every day. He also preaches on occasion and teaches a large adult Sunday school class.

Buck Dozier, former football coach at David Lipscomb High School, is our Youth Director. What a joy it is to have a young man with a fine wife and two sweet little children to give his full time to teaching, helping, assisting, and leading our young people. A youth director can be one of the busiest men anywhere, and his work can be so productive. Our youth director is also head of our Junior and Senior High

Sunday school department, our Wednesday night program, our camp program, and most all activities relating to the young people.

Jerry Sherrill is our Minister of Visitation and a most remarkable man. He serves as general supervisor of our staff. When you have 35 people working on the church staff, somebody has to check them in and out, and keep up with vacations, etc. Jerry is one of those men who can do everything well. He supervises our records room, our information desk, makes the announcements at all services, keeps up with all the people in the hospitals, and makes sure that everybody is visited. He arranges singing for funerals, visits the funeral homes, sees that the family has the preacher they want to do the service, and assists in a thousand ways. He also handles the finances for our television ministry. He knows the congregation well and loves them much, and is a remarkable, detailed man.

George Goldtrap serves as our Minister of Broadcast Media. He is Executive Producer of our television program, handles the syndication of it and at the same time fills in as song leader, as substitute teacher in our large classes, and in other important duties. He is a professional when it comes to radio and television, having had years of experience as a professional announcer and weatherman. He loves the Lord and loves the church and delights in using his expertise in the field of broadcasting. He directs two full time secretaries and several volunteers in the answering of television mail, and keeps our elders informed and up to date on all matters pertaining to our television and radio work.

Norman Slate is our Minister of Personal Evangelism. He is a dynamic young man who was reared in this congregation and understands the Bus Ministry and the importance of home Bible study. He knows how to work within the framework of the unity of the spirit in the bond of peace. He is tractful and dedicated, and like our other ministers has a wife that is so talented and helpful. Norman Slate does not feel threatened by any of our ministers, and none of our ministers feel threatened by him. There is so much work to be done and everybody can have all they can and are willing to do.

The Dilemma

One of the dilemmas the local church finds itself in after it is fortunate enough to build a team is: how in the world do you keep them at home? This is a real problem.

I have become convinced over a period of many years of study and observation that continuity is essential to the building of the local church. A few years ago the Madison church and one of our great sister congregations in Texas were running equal in Bible school attendance. One Sunday we would have more, the next Sunday they would have more. However, we outgrew them, and at one point almost doubled their attendance. The minister had me for breakfast one day with a group of the elders and asked me point blank: "Tell us what happened. Why is it that just a few years ago we both had a Bible school the same size? What happened?" I told him in one word, "Continuity." I explained that in the last few years the local congregation there had changed ministers five times, while the Madison church during those years had continuity.

We have learned that you cannot build in absentia, and you cannot build a local church running around all over the country telling everybody else how to do it. The truth of it is, if you are gone too much the job just is not done at home. This is not only true in ministers of the pulpit, but is true also of every man on the team.

A few years ago I heard a man speak on personal evangelism. I was so fired up and enthusiastic after those great speeches that I made a trip of many miles to visit the speaker's home congregation to study their program of personal evangelism. To my chagrin when I got there one of the elders explained they really did not have a program of personal evangelism. He explained their minister was so busy going to and fro in the land explaining why and how it should be done, that they simply did not have any time to build a program at home.

Now the real truth is the more talented your team, and the more aggressive and dynamic work they do, the more they are in demand. Many of them are young men and feel if they turn down an invitation they will never receive another one. They are not yet mature enough to know that if you are doing the job and you turn them down, it makes them want you that much worse.

76

I do not know the answer to this dilemma, because none of us wants to build a team that no one else would want, but I do have a suggestion. At Madison, we have a policy that if you have been there ten years, you get two weeks vacation. After you have been there twenty years, you get four Sunday vacations. Our elders give our preachers three Sundays to hold meetings. For example, if you get three Sundays of vacation and three Sundays for meetings, that gives you six Sundays a year to be gone. Now six Sundays out of 52 is a pretty big slice if a great program is underway. The only thing I have known to work is after a member of our staff has been gone his allotted Sundays, then his salary is docked and he is paid nothing for the time he is gone.

We once had a song leader that we could not keep at home. Every time we turned around this talented man was gone. We tried to explain that someone had to keep the store. We could not kill the goose that laid the golden egg. We had to do the job at home. After all else failed, the elders adopted the policy of deducting his salary for the time he was gone. In other words, instead of subsidizing his leaving he was paid nothing after the allotted number of Sundays. It caught his attention real quick, and he soon saw that to support his family he had best follow the instructions of those who have the oversight.

We emphasize of course that this policy should be applied fairly and across the board. The larger the program, the more missionaries supported, the more orphan children cared for, and the greater the intensity of the educational program, the greater necessity

77

it is for someone to be at home taking care of the sometimes unexciting but very necessary tasks.

An Old Warhorse is Invaluable

In addition to the ministers I have mentioned on our team, we have three old warhorses. These men have each preached the gospel for over 50 years, and they are such a blessing. It has been our custom through the years at the Madison church to always have at least one preacher on our staff who has borne the battle in the heat of the day. We need his maturity and his Bible knowledge and his wisdom. We are not in the least fearful of a man on our staff who has been a Bible scholar for many years and has proven over and over his loyalty to New Testament Christianity. We want to preach the truth, and we appreciate older men who love it and will help us in the work of the Lord.

Cecil Wright is our writing evangelist. He has preached the gospel for over 50 years and taught for many years at Freed-Hardeman College. He has the largest office of any minister on our staff. It is next door to the author's office, and he has the best private religious library we know of in our brotherhood. What a joy to have a resident writing evangelist available to all of us to discuss the Word of God, to explain difficult passages, and to offer us his wisdom accumulated through years of study.

C. J. Garner is in his early 80s and has preached the gospel for over 50 years. He preached here in Madison and in Old Hickory for 19 years, and served congregations across our brotherhood. He and his wife Sarah direct our library, teach classes and work in our benevolent program. He is known and loved and respected by the entire community. It is such a joy to have him at all the services and to have him live near the church building.

Our third old timer has also preached the gospel for over 50 years and is the well respected R. C. Walker, Sr. R. C. Walker and his gracious wife Elizabeth Showalter Walker have operated our Bible Correspondence school for years. They direct a group of volunteers that grade papers and have taught thousands through the mail. R. C. Walker, Sr. teaches a class for senior citizens, and boosts and supports the program here.

One thing I have noticed about these older preachers is the encouragement they offer to all preachers and teachers in the congregation. It means something when a man who has preached the gospel for over 50 years puts his hand on your shoulder and compliments a sermon. We urge our young people to know and love these older men and to feel free to seek their counsel and advice. It seems to us such a bargain to have an older preacher or two on your staff. Most of them are happy to work for the salary the government allows Social Security recipients to receive. With a small salary from the church and their Social Security they are able to live in dignity, and especially so if the church furnishes them a home. We can truthfully say through the years that having older preachers on our team has proven a resounding and happy success.

79

steps to keep in mind in building your team of ministers as the local congregation becomes strong numerically and financially.

1. Remember that not every preacher can fit into a team situation. Do not employ a preacher whose ego will not permit him to be one of a team. You are asking for disaster and trouble.

2. Have the responsibility of each preacher in writing and the job description clearly understood so there are no hard feelings or misunderstandings.

3. Make sure that every minister understands that we all work together in peace and harmony and love, and that nothing, and I mean nothing, can be tolerated that would destroy this atmosphere. If any preacher is unhappy and cannot fit in, he must fold his tent and leave.

4. We would add one more suggestion. In the congregations we know that have used the team ministry so successfully, they generally have a leader. No preacher should be employed to work on that team that the leader does not have confidence in our who is jealous or envious in any way of the lead preacher. For example, Paul Rogers has been at the Centerville, Tennessee, congregation for a quarter of a century. He is loved and respected and looked to by everybody as far as we know in the entire county and region. It would be catastrophic and unthinkable for those good elders to bring in a preacher who could not work with Paul in peace and harmony. It would be a disservice to the man they brought in, a disservice to Paul Rogers, and could be catastrophic for the ongoing of the kingdom of God in that place.

C	H	A	P	T	E	R	1	1

Suffer Little Children

It was my happy privilege for a quarter of a century to work with the venerable and inimitable Stan Lillie. He was one of the greatest elders and one of the most intelligent men I have ever known. He was a master in church work and a genuine shepherd. He was personnel man for many years at Dupont, and he knew everyone who worked at the Old Hickory plant by memory and could give you a run down on their family. He knew every member of the Madison church, the wife's name, her maiden name, the children's names, the dog's name and their family history. He was in the home of every member, and for many years our records office was inside Stan Lillie's head.

He worked alongside another giant, J. Lindsay Hunter. J. L. Hunter was a remarkable man. He was small of stature, but a spiritual giant. He went to Burritt College with A. R. Holton and other Bible scholars and was a brilliant church historian. The unusual and remarkable thing about J. L. Hunter was his vision and optimism. At 80, he seemed unafraid to plan ahead and launch out into the deep. He could very well have used his influence to have stifled and stagnated the work at Madison. If he and Stan Lillie had been fearful, it would have created fear in the rest of us. I often told J. Lindsay Hunter that in point of years he was our oldest elder and in point of vision our youngest.

A congregation with a balanced program that expects to grow ought to go all out for the children.

Among the many things that these two grand old men taught was the importance of looking after the children. Stan Lillie believed that the younger a child was, the more important it was to have the proper training and facilities. He told me on several occasions: "Now commissioner, I want you to remember that to build a great church you must start with the children. You can't do much with us old people. We are set in our ways and not prone to much get up and go. However, remember you can teach the children, and let us do everything we can to provide a teaching program and a Sunday school that will be absolutely excellent in every way."

I believe a balanced New Testament church will not forget the little ones. They are small for such a short time; they will not wait. If we do not take care of them immediately it will be too late. It is sad to see little children in a classroom that is dull and damp and

82

dreary, and maybe sitting on a bench where their little feet cannot reach the ground. It is so wonderful to see a classroom with the proper sized chair that is bright and cheerful and happy in appearance with bulletin boards that blaze with enthusiasm and the joy of the Christian religion.

Outside of the Sunday school, a Bible kindergarten program in the church building is one method of taking care of those little children. It has been Madison's privilege for 30 years to have a first class A-1 kindergarten for boys and girls three, four and five years of age. Our teachers are so dedicated and work for such a small salary that we strive to make up in recognition what we lack in financial support. Each child pays a small tuition if he is able, and some who are unable to pay are given scholarships. Many of our successful young professionals in the congregation have received a running start in their school work with the loving training at our Bible kindergarten.

Another program that recognizes the importance of the children is our Thursday School. It is sometimes called a Mothers Day Out. The purpose of the school is to provide our mothers with at least one day a week for time of their own. The school is operated for all pre-school children ages 30 days to six years, and runs concurrently with the school year. I remember a few years ago counseling with a young lady who was on the verge of a nervous breakdown. She had four pre-school children, and I asked her if she had one day a week she could call her own and rest and be prepared to do a better job as a mother and a wife. She replied that on her husband's salary she had not had one day out on her own since she had married six years ago.

Madison decided to do something about this situation and others in the congregation. We were delighted to find there were mothers who would be happy to teach a school one day a week. We told all our young mothers to bring all the children they had to the church building on Thursday, and we would take care of them, teaching them the Bible and showing loving care. It has been such a blessing to the children, but most of all it has been a blessing to young mothers.

I can truthfully say as I look back on my own life that the most difficult period was when we had preschool children. It is a time when you are just getting started, there is not enough money for a babysitter, and the stress and strain of being cooped up with children seven days a week, 365 days a year is just not too good.

Stan Lillie also taught us not to forget the importance of the arrival of a new baby. We announce it from the pulpit, put it in the bulletin, and pay a visit to that home. If it is a boy baby we take it a blue New Testament, and if it is a girl baby we take a pink New Testament. We tell those young parents that we have a first class cradle roll department, operated primarily by grandmothers and mothers, and that we can take care of their baby in Sunday school. It is tragic that a young lady goes to Sunday school for 20 years, marries and has a baby and takes the excuse of this little one to quit coming to Sunday morning Bible school. Now, when she needs God worse than any time in her life, she gets out of the life-long habit that would be such a blessing to her.

Some of us have struggled with a couple of babies during the worship service of the church and know how exasperating it can be. It is so simple to have well-equipped nurseries, staffed by qualified mothers and grandmothers at every service of the church. The young father and mother can leave their baby in good hands while they enjoy the worship service. When the child gets big enough to behave and to not cause distraction, then he can sit with the family in the main auditorium. We have even provided glass enclosed training rooms with pews where the service can be heard, so that parents can train the toddler to behave in the worship service.

The point I am trying to make is simply this: a congregation with a balanced program that expects to grow ought to go all out for the children. I like the story of two city boys who visited their grandmother on the farm. One day they were trying to get the old family cow in the barn, and after about an hour they were ready to give up. A young country boy was sitting on the fence, and he began to laugh at them and told them that it was really funny that two big boys could not even get one old cow in the barn. The city boys said they would like to see him get the cow in the barn and they reminded him if he did not they were going to give him a first class whipping. The country boy said, "Get out of the lot, it's no problem at all." He went in the lot and ignored the cow. He took hold of her little calf and put it in the barn, and here came the cow, lickety-split. When he took care of the calf, he gave the greatest incentive in the world to the cow to come in. How many thousands have been won to the church, and how many more thousands strengthened because the congregation was very sensitive to little children.

"Suffer the little children to come unto me, and forbid them not: for of such is the kingdom of heaven."

A Leader In The
Worship Service Will Help

A leader in the worship service can be most helpful. It has been my observation over a period of many years that congregations that are growing are those who have a worship service that is enthusiastic, optimistic, cheerful, delightful and happy. The congregation whose service is dead, slow, cold, formal, and shows no enthusiasm is a congregation that has probably already reached its potential years ago.

The question is, can we have an enthusiastic, happy and enjoyable worship service and still be scriptural and absolutely Biblical? Our answer to that question is a resounding and emphatic yes. We believe the worship service of the New Testament church was a celebration. It was a celebration of the greatest event known in human history, namely the resurrection of Jesus. Is it any wonder that we call it the Gospel, that is the Good News? In the resurrection of Christ we have the greatest news ever known to mortal man. The apostle Paul teaches us, "if Christ be not raised from the dead, we are of all men most miserable." If there is no resurrection then our preaching is vain, our labor is vain, and we are without hope in this world. Everything we hold near and dear in hope and promise of eternal life depends on the resurrection of Jesus.

Now since the resurrection of our Lord is celebrated at every Sunday morning service in our songs and sermons and the Lord's Supper, why shouldn't the service have an air of celebration and joy and happiness? Why should the Sunday morning service not be an uplifting, and delightful experience? I believe it should, and indeed I believe it ought to be. A dull, disorganized service is not very uplifting, and is not conducive to growth.

The question is, can we have an enthusiastic, happy and enjoyable worship service and still be scriptural and absolutely Biblical?

I believe it is wise to have one man presiding over the worship services and I want to share a few observations that I believe will be helpful. If the brother who begins the service is optimistic and really knows what he is doing, he can set the tone for a great worship service. When he greets the people and gives the order of worship, he does it with a sense of joy. A qualified person leading the worship service can avoid several distractions that are too common. For example, he can avoid the repetition of announcements that become so boring. We have seen services where the announcements were given just before the service began, and then repeated at the close of the service. It is so irritating to see brethren take so long to close a service, especially when everyone in the audience knows that the service has run overtime. Instead of increasing the effectiveness of the service, it has done the very opposite.

Talking Songleader

Another pitfall that can be avoided by the man presiding is the talking song leader. Some services last too long because the song leader is really a frustrated preacher. He cannot simply announce the number of the song and lead us in it, he must explain what simple words mean, and tell some of us who have been singing this song for 50 years what it means. In other words, there is a sermonette between each song, causing the service to go on and on and the effectiveness and joy to go down and down.

When Charles Nelson led singing for a decade at the Madison church, I had an agreement with him. Charles Nelson is one of the finest men I have ever known and one of the most talented singers in the nation. Half jokingly I told him if he would not preach, I would not lead singing, but if he started preaching between every song, I was going to start leading the singing. He told me that the agreement suited him absolutely to perfection, and he always kept his side of the bargain.

Avoid Dead Space

Those of us who are experienced with radio and television know how important it is to avoid what the broadcasters term "dead space." Thirty seconds of silence on a television program can be devastating. If you note a well-produced television program, the picture will change every six seconds, and there is absolutely no dead space. So many times in a service the brother that is going to lead the prayer sits halfway back in the auditorium, gets up, walks all the way down to the front, and gets in the pulpit to lead the prayer. The people are sitting there waiting for him to get down and to lead the prayer. It would be so simple if those who were going to lead the prayer would be on the front seat or on the stage, and when we get ready to pray there would not be any wasted motion and time. We have had little or no instruction in the church on these matters that we are discussing, and to some they will seem trivial, but I believe they are important. The congregation that has a reputation of a service that keeps moving and is a real celebration of the good news of Jesus, will find that their own members will be coming back and that new people will be enjoying the service.

The point I am trying to make is simply this: A worship service can be exciting and spiritual, and at the same time be absolutely scriptural. We can sing the songs in the spirit and attitude that they should be sung. The singing can be a delightful, moving, and happy experience. The sermon can be uplifting and Biblical and encourage us in the good news of Jesus. The Lord's Supper can and should be a most meaningful experience—maybe the sweetest ten minutes of the entire week. The reading of the Bible and the prayers can inspire us and uplift us. With a little thought and effort we can organize a worship service that will be as far from being dull as the north pole is from the south pole. I challenge you to visit some of the congregations that are beginning to reach the peak of their potential in growth and ask you to note that every single one of those churches without a single exception will have a worship service that is a celebration of the greatest news known to mortal man, and everyone of them will have a service that is uplifting. Note the joy in the singing, the relevant, biblical message, the absence of needless dead space and lost motion, and that the service moves and flows as they sing, pray, preach, observe the Lord's Supper, and lay by and store.

A Typical Sunday Morning Worship Service

I have been requested to share a typical Sunday morning worship service at the Madison church. We have no choice but to facilitate and organize a service, because we are forced to use our plant four times each Sunday morning, worship at 8 a.m., Sunday school at 9, Bible school again at 10, and worship at 11. Those who come to worship at 8 o'clock go to Bible school at 9, and those that come to Bible school at 10 o'clock go to worship at 11. This enables us to use the entire plant twice on Sunday morning. It is already heated in the winter and already cooled in the summer, and this arrangement of duplicate services and duplicate Bible schools saves the church hundreds of thousands of dollars, and at the same time makes available hundreds of thousands of dollars for missionaries, for the poor and for the homeless.

91

I am not saying that this format is the only way to do it. As long as the scriptural items of worship are enclosed, I understand it makes no difference whether you have the Lord's Supper before the sermon or after the sermon and I understand it makes no difference whether the collection is taken first or last. I am sharing the format in the hopes that it might be helpful to other growing churches.

At five minutes until eight or five minutes until eleven, two of our preachers come down on the stage. One of them gets the crowd's attention and then presents the other to give the announcements. Jerry Sherrill, who works in visitation, gives the announcements. The reasons we have the same one give them each Sunday are many, but one is that he is familiar with the names and can read them clearly and rapidly. People like to hear their own names pronounced correctly. In giving the announcements Jerry Sherrill mentions the names of the various hospitals. He does not give the room numbers, for that detail can be secured in the bulletin. We generally have a full five minutes of announcements mentioning the names of members in a dozen hospitals or so. The reason we make the announcements is not only for information but to promote the care and concern among our members. The arrival of new babies, the death of a loved one, illness in the family, all are important events, and we feel the local congregation should not be too busy to take note of that in a public way. At the close of the announcements the preacher, generally Brother Jim Mankin, our associate, has all the visitors stand and gives special recognition to them. After this we ask everyone to stand before we start the service and each one to shake hands with everybody in front of them, behind them, to their left, to their right, introduce themselves and say something nice. We are working for friendliness and love and care and against a cold, formal atmosphere. While everyone shakes hands, I (as a rule) come out on the pulpit and everyone gets quiet and sits down. I state again how happy we are to have everybody and give the order of worship—who will lead the singing, who will lead the prayer, who will preside at the Lord's table, then the sermon, the invitation, the Lord's day collection, and the closing prayer. Once the minister gets that service in his hand he never turns it loose. He sees that the service flows freely without dead space, and yet without an appearance of any hurry. After the invitation song the Lord's day collection is taken.

The Lord's day collection is taken last for several reasons. One is, the sermon that day might be on giving, and it is a mark of wisdom to pass the collection plate after the heart has been softened with a Bible message. I really believe many congregations have lost hundreds of dollars and in some cases thousands of dollars because they pass the basket before the sermon.

Now, it is all right to sing an invitation song thirty minutes after the sermon, but we doubt the wisdom of it. In fact when we are holding a revival meeting we do not even like for thirty seconds to take place from the time the sermon ends until we are singing an invitation song. Small things like this may seem to many just trivial and insignificant. However, sometimes the difference between the ordinary and the extraordinary is a few extras and a little common sense. If the worship service is really as important as we have claimed it to be, then why shouldn't it be decent and in order, and why shouldn't we use our best talent and training to help the service be everything in the sight of God that it could be?

Some have suggested that one reason we have lost a few of our young people to the charismatic movement is because they feel starved for warmth and joy in a service they deem to be sterile. I believe we can have an enthusiastic and happy worship service with great feeling and love and yet be true to every Biblical principle and teaching.

I will have to admit that I have received letters from some of our young people over the years that have caused me concern. It has not been uncommon sometimes to receive a letter that says in essence: "We are settled in our school work (or job) and like the climate and the people here, but we have had one disappointment. The church seems to be so inactive and lukewarm. We got our children ready for Sunday school today, and would you believe it—it took us four hours to take those little ones to Sunday school and worship and get home and we only live three or four minutes from the church building. The brethren announced, and announced, and announced, and then got up before they dismissed and announced again. The songs were draggy, and the atmosphere was more of a cemetery or a funeral than a great worship service. We shall strive to do as you have taught us and be loyal and faithful, and hope maybe

94

some day we can have a worship service that is well organized and uplifting. It is so frustrating to wrestle with all these children when you know the long drawn out service could be so much more effective with just a little common sense organization."

On the other hand, we occasionally see a letter like the following that encourages us: "Dear ones: We are settled in our new home, and new job and schools, and you will be glad to know we are very happy. We are especially happy with the church situation here. The congregation is warm and friendly, and the atmosphere is near perfection. When we go to Sunday school at 9 a.m. we know it will be over at 10, and we will be ready for worship. When we start worship at 10, we know that at 11 we will be going home to eat our noon meal and to get the children ready for their rest. We look forward to coming back on Sunday evening, and we do not feel imposed upon. The sermon is well prepared and well organized and executed. The congregation is not as large as we are used to, but as you have taught us it is the spirit and the atmosphere and the scripturalness that really count."

A Going Church
Is A Growing Church

The marching orders of the church of our Lord are given in the Great Commission, and every loyal congregation is very interested in carrying out the Master's command to, "Go ye into all the world, and preach the gospel to every creature. He that believeth and is baptized shall be saved; but he that believeth not shall be condemned."

Continuity in the building of any local congregation is so important and so difficult to maintain.

Paul told Timothy that the church is the pillar and the ground of the truth (I Timothy 3:15). The truth does not depend upon the church for its veracity but it does depend on the church for its proclamation. The church is to uphold the gospel and to proclaim it to all the world.

It would be hard to imagine a congregation that is growing that does not believe in mission work. Sometimes we may be disappointed in some of our efforts, but we must not grow weary in well doing. It is ours to cultivate and to water and to plant—it is God's to give the increase.

I believe it is imperative to keep the congregation informed on the mission program. This takes a conscious effort on the part of many people, but it can be done. We note that many growing churches see that their missionaries, wherever they are in the world, are visited each year and that periodically they are brought home where the people who support them can touch them and see them and associate with them and know them.

In some congregations various classes adopt a missionary and write them and their family. If the missionary has children in the eighth grade, then those youngsters of the same age in the home congregation are pen pals. It is vital that the missionary get from the sponsoring congregation more than just a check.

A few years ago it was my privilege to lead a group of 43 people to visit churches of Christ in Europe. One missionary told us this sad story. He said, "I am deeply appreciative of the people back home supporting me. However, I wish so much they would write me and come to see me and keep in touch. The only thing I hear from them is a check each month."

One technique that is used by some of the growing congregations is each year to have a missionary seminar. For this seminar the missionaries are brought home, and teach large adult classes, appear in the assembly, and are seen by members of the church. Also during the weekend program, are scheduled men

98

who have expertise in the mission field to discuss various problems and offer suggested solutions. We have found this mission seminar each year to be a delightful boost to our mission work. It enables members of the congregation to feel a vital part of the program and to know of it first hand from the missionaries.

Disappointed but not Discouraged

It is inevitable that we suffer some disappointments in our mission work because we are dealing with human beings, but let us not be discouraged. One of the greatest disappointments Madison has experienced is our inability to find missionaries to stay on the job and with the job until a self-supporting church emerges. Sometimes it takes two, three, or four men before a congregation becomes self-supporting, and each time he leaves the work is set back. We hear over and over again that: "I'm going to this city to give my life to building a local church that is self-supporting." And yet again and again and again there are greener pastures. Some problems come up, and alas the missionary is gone. Continuity in the building of any local congregation is so important and so difficult to maintain.

We have also suffered the heartbreak of disappointment in some of our missionaries. A few years ago two men sold us on helping them go to a great city in a foreign country. They were going to consolidate a couple of small congregations and give their lives to building a great church. We were excited about it and poured several thousand dollars into the work. And yet to our disappointment these men left ancient landmarks and the Bible pattern and went off to the charismatic movement. Instead of working to build a New Testament church, they fizzled and failed. We were disappointed but not discouraged.

On another occasion, we decided to select an American city of 100,000 people that did not have a New Testament church, and to send a couple of missionaries and support them, and help them buy property and stand by the congregation until it could stand on its own. Now theoretically it sounded good, but in actual practice it fizzled and miserably failed. To our consternation and disappointment, the two preachers could not get along. They were unable to keep the unity of the spirit in the bond of peace, even among the small crowd. After investing thousands of dollars and many hours of time, and sending campaign groups to work the city, the building had to be sold, and we had to fold our tents. Thousands of dollars and thousands of man hours had apparently gone down the drain. Yes, we were disappointed but not discouraged.

Along with the disappointments there are success stories that make it all worth while. A few brilliant successes offset a lot of disappointments. A few months ago, we were privileged to visit this missionary who has been supported a number of years by the Madison church. When we arrived in this lovely little city, we found a delightful new church building, located on an excellent lot, and to our surprise and delight the little building was overflowing. They were keeping the unity of the spirit in the bond of peace—they were growing, and the atmosphere was beautiful. At the close of the service a young marine from the nearby base came forward to be baptized. It was a service we will never forget. Our missionary preached him a sermon that was as fine as we have ever heard. The congregation sang "I've got a Mansion just over the Hilltop," and after he was baptized each member walked around, took his hand and fondly embraced him. It was soul stirring and delightful. We found the congregation well respected in this little city. The missionary had a good reputation from those within and without. It was obvious that the congregation was well on its way to being self-supporting. It was rewarding and encouraging.

In doing mission work we must remember that "My word shall not return unto me void." After we use the best judgment we have and zealously support the preaching of the word, we must leave it in the hands of our Heavenly Father.

Go Across the Ocean and Go Across the Street

One of the rewarding things of a mission program in the local congregation is that it encourages us to do mission work at home. The congregation that is interested in going across the ocean is generally also interested in going across the street. I have found that the young people who are willing to go on campaigns to help establish the church where it is not known, are also willing to take a census and to set up Bible studies and to do door to door canvassing in our own community. The word "go" is a key word in Christianity, and the congregation that carries out the command and is faithful to it will be blessed. We have observed it again and again and again—the going church is the growing church. It builds enthusiasm, it increases dedication, it gives great meaning to our church work and it inspires our young people.

In the little congregation in which I was reared, there was a large framed motto on the wall of the Sunday school classroom. It said: "Go ye therefore, and teach all nations, baptizing them in the name of the Father, and of the Son, and of the Holy Spirit: Teaching them to observe all things whatsoever I have commanded you: and lo, I am with you alway, even unto the end of the world" (Matthew 28:19-20). This motto needs to be hung on the walls of our hearts, and may we never forget it.

Three
Perceptive Observations

It has been our privilege to have so many to visit the Madison church and to make helpful and sometimes very perceptive observations. We have been privileged to have thousands and thousands of visiting Bible school teachers, elders, and deacons, and church leaders to spend the weekend in our homes here at Madison and attend our workshops. Currently we are not running these workshops, but for many years we did, and it was a joy to listen to people giving their impressions.

Everybody wants to be an Indian and nobody wants to be a chief.

There are three observations over the years that have stuck with me that I am anxious to share in this book, because they might be of help to someone else.

My father was an elder, a Bible school teacher, and a church leader for many years. He lived 80 miles south of Nashville and visited us quite often. My father knew the Bible and had a head full of common sense. One day after a weekend visit to the Madison church, I asked him to give me his assessment of the work here and to tell me what his impressions were on looking it over closely. Here are two of the observations he made.

Everybody Wants to be an Indian and Nobody Wants to be a Chief

The first observation this down to earth man made was his surprise that everybody was willing to do the menial tasks and nobody wanted to be a boss or tell others what to do. We had just passed our communion room, and there were several members there, including the editor of our metropolitan afternoon paper, who had an apron on. They were washing by hand the communion glasses, and then after sterilizing the glasses, they were filling them. (I'm told that we fill 5,620 individual communion cups each Sunday here at Madison.)

One observation my father had made was the joy and happiness that these people were receiving over spending an hour or two together in such a menial task as washing and drying cups.

"It amazes me that apparently everybody in this congregation wants to be an Indian," he said. "Nothing seems too menial or unimportant for them to do. Now, at home we all want to be chiefs and nobody wants to be an Indian. Everybody has a big, high and mighty plan that they are willing to direct. It may be because in the business world we are supervisors and business men. We tell an employee to go and he goes— we tell him to come and he comes. And this may carry over into our church work. We are all willing to be a chief and propose big plans and tell others what to do, but we don't want to roll up our sleeves and get our own hands dirty."

I have thought of this assessment many times over the last few years. I think it was perceptive and correct. Somehow, someway we must get across the desire to serve. We must understand that he that would be greatest among you must be servant of all. We must come to believe that if it furthers the cause of Christ and is good, then it doesn't make any difference if it is rather mundane and menial.

I believe part of this spirit comes from a sincere desire to see that the job is done and from very little concern, if any, on who gets the credit. What difference does it make who gets the credit as long as the job is done?

I've Never Seen People Enjoy Being Together So Much

The second perception that this man, known for his common sense, and good judgment, shared with me was also one I will never forget. He said I observe every time I come that several groups are together after the service having a meal and talking, visiting, enjoying each other. It seems to me these people never get tired of being together. They look for excuse, apparently, to be together and just talk and visit and eat and sing and just apparently enjoy each other.

105

He was right in that assessment. The beloved John mentions two great blessings in the Christian religion. In I John 1:8 the first great blessing he mentions is the forgiveness of sins, and the second great blessing he mentions in the same passage is the fellowship of kindred minds. I have observed that congregations that grow are those who are able to develop a spirit of joy and happiness at just being together. We need to look for excuses to get to know one another better— to talk to one another—to communicate our care and concern, and just for the sheer enjoyment of fellow Christians. "Blessed be the tie that binds, and how sweet and heavenly is the sight of those that love the Lord" who can just enjoy the sweet fellowship of fellow Christians.

There Is Not Only a Willingness But a Deep Seeded Desire, Almost The Compulsion to Share

The third observation I am sharing with you was given by my distinguished kinsman who has directed the academic program at Oklahoma Christian College for over a quarter of a century—Dr. Ross Stafford North. When Ross Stafford had spent several days with us here at Madison, I asked him to give me the benefit of his observations, what did he think were some strong points, and what would be some suggestions to improve.

He told me that he found an almost unbelievable willingness and happiness in sharing with others. He said, "The fact that you share with any congregation that comes along and any individual that comes along,

106

anywhere, anyplace, anytime you can, has greatly impressed me." He said he had noted among the teachers and supervisors in the Bible school departments, especially, a sheer delight in sharing some means or method with another congregation or another teacher.

Surely any joy is sweeter when you can share it, and any sorrow is less sorrowful when you can share it. I recommend the local congregation show total and complete unselfishness in sharing with sister congregations and with those who stop by just looking around and asking questions.

All Out
For The Young People

One of the important elements in a well-balanced program of work in a growing church is to remember the young people. I am speaking especially in this chapter of the teenage years, or at least from ten to eighteen. The journey from childhood to manhood or womanhood has never been an easy one. There are those who seem to make the journey very smoothly and without catastrophic incident. There are others who seem to have a dreadfully tough time on this journey.

I have observed that congregations that go all out for their young people seem to be the ones that enjoy the greatest growth.

The wise man Solomon said, "Remember now thy Creator in the days of thy youth, while the evil days come not, nor the years draw nigh, when thou shalt say, I have no pleasure in them." The wise man knew how important were these years. It is a time when most young men and women obey the gospel, and it is a time when the twig is bent that determines so much of the future.

In our society today with all its lurking evils for the young, with intoxicating liquor, cigarettes, drugs, pornography, permissiveness, sexual immorality, and other temptations round about, our young people need all the help they can get. Also, our Christian families need all the help they can get.

I have observed that congregations that go all out for their young people seem to be the ones that enjoy the greatest growth. There are so many wholesome activities for young people. Of course a first class Sunday school program is essential. We need our strongest teachers in the Junior High department, for it is this age in which we are prone to lose so many. I am also a great believer in an enthusiastic and dynamic Vacation Bible School. The Vacation Bible School could and should be one of the highlights of the year. It is wise to make VBS one characterized with joy and enthusiasm and happiness. If these young people can grow up in an atmosphere of love and happiness and stability and joy, it is bound to have an excellent influence on their lives in the years ahead.

About 30 years ago Madison decided to take all our young people from ages 10 to 16 to Bible camp each summer for two weeks of intensive training in Bible. We did not have an acre of ground or a penny of money, but only the desire to train these young people. The National Guard and the United States Army

110

have proven that you can do a lot with the young in two weeks' time.

It was our privilege to raise money for six tents among our friends, and we asked the elders' permission for the congregation to have a Bible camp program each summer. Since we had no money we charged each child three dollars to help pay for the groceries, and took a special collection each year asking those to give who believed in young people and were convinced a program of teaching and fellowship such as we were proposing would be a good one. "To him that hath it shall be given, and he shall have abundance." From this humble beginning, it was not long until we owned our own camp, and today just 15 or 20 minutes up the interstate we have Valley View Bible Camp, built by the labor and love of our members, and still supported by one special collection each year. Young men and women are taught the Bible three or four times a day, and they have an excellent opportunity for wholesome and supervised fellowship and activities. Many of the young people learn to swim at camp, learn to ride a horse, and learn to get along with other boys and girls, which is so important.

At the Bible camp every youngster is treated as if he were something very important and special, because of course he is. However it is understood that any child that does not shape up must be shipped out. We have sent home elders' children, preachers' children, deacons' children, and Sunday school teachers' children. It is self-evident from the beginning that no foolishness is tolerated at the Bible camp. Everybody who stays behaves himself and respects authority.

Bible Teaching

Of course our first and foremost concern is that these young people have a solid foundation in the Bible. We have gone all out to provide an excellent teaching program, excellent facilities, and real care and concern about the teaching program. For 18 years my wife and I gave our summers to conducting the Bible camp. This was in the days when we did not have a youth minister. The great reward of working with the young people was the influence on our own children. Those who give their time to young people are blessed and rewarded in the lives of their own youngsters.

Through the years we have used our farm for wiener roasts, treasure hunts, picnics and outings for the young people. Now, it may not seem important to provide fellowship and association for young people, but the truth of it is if we do not provide wholesome activities for the young, they are going to find activity that is unwholesome. It is wonderful when the family is able to provide for the young people, but in our society today with single parents, working mothers, and unchristian influences all around, most parents need all the help they can get.

The Family Life Center

A few years ago, after 20 years of deliberation, our elders came to the decision that we must do something for our young people on a seven-days-a-week, 365-day basis. They came to the conclusion that there are two divine institutions, the home and the church. And while the church does not want to supplant the home, it is both right and wise for the church to aid and support and help the family in every way that is good and right. The elders made the decision to build a family life center. What is a family life center? It is a Sunday school annex that is used for Sunday morning Bible study classes, Sunday evening classes, Wednesday evening classes, and is also open seven afternoons and evenings a week to the glory of God and for the good of young people and to provide a place for young people to be where there is no drinking, no profanity, no drugs, and no pornography.

In some communities the need for such may not be, but in the big city where the community centers are drug infested, where the public school is no longer the ally of a Christian home in high moral standards, and where the streets are not safe and the alleys are dangerous, what are the young people to do?

I am not suggesting that a congregation ought to have a Sunday school annex that can be open seven days and evenings a week if that would cause confusion in the congregation. I have caught considerable flack from among some of our brethren for going all out for the young people and providing this family life center, especially so from our brethren who do not support homes for homeless children or cooperation among churches. The interesting thing is we have not received, as far as I know, one objection or one word of criticism from any member of the Madison church or from any family for providing such marvelous atmosphere and supervision and help for our young families trying to rear their children in a difficult age.

A young woman stopped me at the door a few months ago and told me that her husband had walked out on her and left her with four children to rear, but she said, "I will not give up, and I will not give in. By the grace of God I am going to keep these four children together and rear them in the church. With the elders and members helping me and providing a place where my children can come any afternoon after school or any evening in the whole year and be with other Christian young people, and under the supervision of men and women who are interested in the Lord, I'm going to make it."

Another young man visited the family life building one day when schools were closed because of snow. On his return his mother asked him how things went that day. He told her he had had the most marvelous experience and was really delighted. He said he had spent the day with 300 teenagers down at the church of Christ, and did not hear one four-letter word and did not see one young person become unruly or misbehave. He declared he had never seen young people enjoy themselves so much and have such a good time in a good way.

Some people object that to go all out for young people, keeping them off the streets and away from the drug infested community centers, will work a financial hardship on the church. I can understand how this could be, but it has not proven so in Madison's

114

case. Our members gave one Sunday in cash $462,000 to build the annex. That was an indication of how badly they wanted it and how they were willing to sacrifice to pay for it. While the entire building is under the supervision of our Youth Minister, Buck Dozier, the parents volunteer to give their time in supervising and helping.

Another objection to going all out for the young people in this regard is that the tail may wag the dog, and that there may be more interest in providing Christian fellowship and association for young people than in edification, teaching, mission work and benevolent work. Our answer to this is we have not found this to be so. Everyone understands that our primary purpose is to teach the word of God, to build Christian character, to edify, and to preach the gospel. Providing an opportunity for our young people to be together and for peer pressure to be in the direction of righteousness has not in any way hindered our program of work.

We would like to emphasize that it took us 20 years to make the decision to build this annex for the young people. Paul tells Titus in Titus 3:1, "to be ready to every good work." We came to the conclusion that supporting our Christian families and providing for our young people was indeed a good work.

One of our ministers visited a congregation in another state recently, and some children were on the parking lot playing basketball and having a good time. The minister of the congregation remarked that he just could not go along with an annex that was open seven days a week for young people. Our friend replied, "the only difference between what you have in the parking lot and what we have, is that ours has a roof over it." One of our friends in Florida made the remark when the congregation was having a delightful picnic and basket dinner in the backyard on a beautiful sunny day on January 1—"Brother North, this back yard is our family life center." I replied, "It is a mighty good one, and it is wonderful to see the people of God have an opportunity to be together and love each other, and know each other and associate one with the other."

I am aware that in different sections of our country congregations have different practices about the use of their building. I have no intention of causing confusion and division over this. For example, in some sections there is objection to eating, to having a basket dinner in the building, or having a fellowship room, or classrooms that can be put together for an old fashioned basket dinner. To us such an objection is really ridiculous. My grandfather and great-grandfather, Ira North, Jr. and Ira North, Sr. preached at little country churches in Lawrence County, Tennessee, and held gospel meetings. On the Lord's Day they would preach and then go out under the trees on the church yard and spread the dinner and enjoy a delightful fellowship together. If a cloud came up and it rained, they came in the main auditorium, turned the pews around facing each other, spread the dinner on the pews, and everybody enjoyed the meal without getting wet. Following the meal, they cleared the pews, turned them around, and that afternoon had singing and preaching. But, my grandfather and great-grandfather knew the Bible from "In the beginning" in Genesis to "Amen" in Revelation, and they knew that the building was not the church. They knew and preached, "The kingdom of God is within you." And they knew that the church was the saved, the called out, the redeemed, the people. It does seem sad to us that brethren who have a water fountain, a restroom in the building, and a coffee pot in the preacher's office throw up their hands in holy horror when members of the church meet together in sweet fellowship for a basket dinner.

However, I want to emphasize that nothing, and I mean absolutely nothing, should disturb the unity of the spirit in the bond of peace. Let the minority give in to the majority in all matters of judgment. We must get along and love each other and boost each other, and give in on matters of judgment. In matters of faith we are one, in matters of opinion let there be liberty, and in all things let there be love. Now having said all that, I want to say—in my judgment—how wise and wonderful is that congregation in the big city, where parents have such a tremendous task saving their children, when the local congregation says we believe in the family. We believe the family is of God. We will aid and support the family in every way that we can. We will help you see that your children always have places to go that are wholesome and companions that are Christian.

Of course, one of the great benefits and joys of going all out for the young people is to see them meet and marry each other and rear their children in the nurture and admonition of the Lord. Hundreds of our

117

own young people, yea we believe most of our young people, marry within the local congregation—and those who do have a great and glorious chance to build a stable, united Christian home. There is no way to take the risk out of marriage, and no way to guarantee that our young people will marry as we wish or turn out as we wish, but we are convinced the local congregation, next to the family itself, can do so much to lessen the risk and to lower the odds of our precious young people being lost to the church and the cause of Christ.

I urge each congregation on its own, working within the framework of the unity of the spirit in the bond of peace, to go all out for your young people. Give time and money and effort and prayer to the young people. The young are young for such a short time. They make so many decisions in such a short time that will influence a lifetime. The time to reach them and solidify their faith is when they are young. Let us go all out for the young people.

C H A P T E R   1 6

Minority Rule
Will Seal Your Doom

I want to mention one evil and vice in church work that can cause so much heartache and sorrow. I believe the policy is so inherently evil and wrong that it will guarantee the demise of any congregation and will make sure that growth is absolutely impossible.

Let everybody have his say and nobody have his way all the time.

I am speaking of the Hitler and Stalin attitude of minority rule. Now, in the New Testament church every congregation had its own elders who had the oversight, and its own deacons who served under the elders, as did the evangelistic teachers. However, some congregations have adopted the policy that if one person objects to anything, any matter of expediency, the congregation will not do it. Can you imagine in your wildest dreams any successful American Corporation saying that anytime one stock holder disa-

119

greed on matters of judgment and expediency they would not go with the idea? This gives the brother who is born in the objective case and kickative mood a Stalin veto over every suggestion that is made.

I mention this point because I am convinced that such a policy error in the local congregation is so serious that it seals the doom of that church insofar as it ever being a growing and dynamic congregation.

Of course, if any elder or deacon or teacher or member wants to object, let them be heard. Let everybody have his say and nobody have his way all the time. In other words, when the dust settles, in matters of expediency the minority must give in to the majority, or else we have minority rule, and the Biblical principle of "let every man esteem the other better than himself" is completely destroyed.

His Natural Gait

I love the story told by the late A. C. Dunkleberger, who was an elder here at the Madison church for years, and edited the daily afternoon paper. He said that many years ago a man on the square here in Davidson County in Nashville traded for a horse and buggy. He was careful to ask if the horse was well broken, etc. He was assured that the horse was broken and that he was a fine buggy horse; just exactly what he needed. After such assurance, he paid for the horse and buggy, sat in the buggy, and started home across the river to Madison. Just as soon as he was in the buggy, the horse started running away, and for many miles he ran as hard as he could before

120

the new owner was finally able to stop him. The next day he took the horse back to the seller and explained what happened, and told him that he was given the assurance that the horse was broken. The seller just gave a brush of his hand and said, "Oh well, think nothing of it. Running away is just his natural gait."

Finding fault and criticizing, killing good ideas, and shooting down worthy programs is just a normal gait for some brethren. They are born in the objective case and kickative mood and are just naturally against everything.

Now, one of these good brethren can be tolerated without complete despair when you know that he is not likely to carry the day. After more level-headed and sensible brethren have spoken up, then everything may be all right. However, to place a Stalin veto in the hands of such a brother is absolutely unthinkable.

I would recommend to every young preacher in America to be sure and check this policy out before you accept work as a minister of the local church. If the brethren have the minority rule policy, you can know that the doom of that congregation is sealed and your work cannot be either pleasant, happy, or successful.

I have seen hundreds and thousands and tens of thousands of decisions made here at the Madison church over the last 31 years. I have seen every person in leadership graciously give in when it was evident that he was standing practically alone. The Bible teaches us in honor to prefer one another. We must learn to have our say without becoming upset and

121

mad and pouty because we are unable to rule with an iron hand. It is so beautiful to see men in leadership positions able to make hundreds of decisions and move a great work ahead. It is frustrating and intolerable to see a great work scuttled and killed because of an unconscionable policy of minority rule.

How Do You Do Things
When You Don't Have Any Money?

Ishudder when I think of the multiplied hundreds and hundreds of good, scriptural, sound, wonderful programs that have been killed in so many local churches with the simple expression: "We ain't got no money."

Of course, Jesus teaches us to count the cost and we are to use good, sound judgment, but the simple truth is when a program of work is scriptural, sound and needed, and we are convinced that God wants it done, a way can be found. I want to share just three illustrations of monumental programs that have been preeminently successful and have accomplished untold good, and yet were begun without any money.

Some 25 years ago Madison learned there were thousands of homeless children in our country who were unloved, unwanted and uncared for. Realizing a part of pure religion before God is to take care of these homeless children (according to James 1:27) we determined to start a program for homeless children.

As I look back it seems strange that we would have such noble ambitions when we did not have an acre of ground or a penny of money.

We had a little basement building—not even a decent auditorium in which to worship—and our elders appointed 11 men, full of faith and the Holy Spirit, and asked them to do an in-depth study on the problem and suggest something that we as a congregation could do to really get involved in the practice of pure and undefiled religion. After a couple of years of study, they recommended that we build a beautiful new home, four bedrooms, two baths, put a young father and mother in it, and six homeless children. Our elders thought this a great idea, but we did not have a dime. It just seems that God provides and wonderful and mysterious and glorious things happen to a church that is determined to practice as well as preach pure and undefiled religion.

The simple truth is when a program of work is scriptural, sound and needed, and we are convinced that God wants it done, a way can be found.

I made a visit to one of our old-time members. She was a dear old maid, and owned a subdivision near the Madison church. I visited her with fear and trepidation. She was a little peculiar and had a big dog. I went in the office and prayed for the Lord to guide my old stumbling lips and help me to say the right thing in the right way. I felt brave and went to see Miss Opha. However, I almost lost my nerve when I

walked up on the porch and that big dog came to the
door. Miss Opha invited me in and asked me what I
wanted. I told her I was fearful and hesitant, because
I was afraid I would say the wrong thing. She told
me not to just stand there but to get on with it and
say what I had on my mind, and then I told her, "We
want you to give up your subdivision and let us use
it to take care of homeless children." She threw back
her head and laughed, and this frightened me. I fig-
ured that I had blown it. However, after the laughter
subsided, she said seriously: "You can have it. I have
always wanted it used for the glory of God, the good
of the church. Send old Brother Lillie up here and a
lawyer, and we'll work out the details."

Now here we were with a beautiful subdivision, a
great desire to take care of homeless children, and no
money. So I asked the elders if we could pass the
basket in the Sunday morning Bible classes and say
something like this: "You have a home, you have a
father and mother, you have nice clothes, and you
have a good school to attend. Will you give a little bit
extra each Sunday morning in this class that we may
provide some little boy or some little girl with a loving
father and mother, nice clothes, a good place to go
to school, and a Christian home in which to live?"
When I proposed this to the elders, Stan Lillie said,
"How much do you think we need to get this program
started?" My reply was about $600 per week. He re-
plied, "I think we will get it, but it will hurt our regular
contribution of $300 per Sunday." I asked Brother
Lillie if it took a Ph.D. in mathematics to figure out
that if we got $600 a Sunday in the Bible classes and

the regular contribution did go down $300 we would still be ahead. And after all, what difference does it make? It is the same Lord's day, the same elders, the same treasurer, the same congregation, and if the man is healed on the Sabbath, or on some other day, what difference does it make? Brother Lillie replied, "It doesn't make any difference," and he said, as he did so often, "there is just one answer to this—let's give it a try. If it works, that will be wonderful, and if it doesn't, we will try something else."

Not only did it work, but the success has been phenomenal, heartwarming, and wonderful. The Bible classes in this one congregation have contributed $2,245,902.61 for the care of homeless children. Over a thousand boys and girls have enjoyed a Christian foster father and mother in an entire, well-rounded child care program for the homeless, including foster care, social services, cottage care, and adoption, which has been joyfully, happily financed.

I often think of all these children who have been reared in the church and blessed in so many ways, and then think what would it have been like if our elders had turned down this simple plan of finance? Not only would hundreds of children not have received the blessing, but thousands of Christians who have been involved in the program might not have been involved. And today, as this book goes to press, the Bible classes are giving $150,000 per year to support homeless children. The surprise has been that the regular contribution not only did not fall $300, it is now $25,000 per week more than it was when the child care program started. It is just another illustration of where there is a genuine desire, the finances will come.

Here is another illustration of a successful and happy work that was started without a penny. Over a quarter of a century ago, I asked the elders if we could take every boy and girl in the congregation away during the summer to Short Mountain Camp in Woodbury, Tennessee, and then give them a period of intensive training in the Bible. The United States Army has proven that you can impart a tremendous amount of information in a very short time if the necessity and will to do so is there. Our elders listened carefully but came up with a sensible answer, and that is, "we ain't got no money."

My answer to that was this: "I will give my time to directing it, and our Sunday school teachers will give their vacation to helping us, we will charge each child a small fee for food if they can afford it, and if not we will take them free of charge. We can do all this if you will permit us to pass the basket one time a year on Sunday morning after the regular contribution, and ask people to make a special sacrifice to teach our children the Bible in the Bible camp."

Stan Lillie asked one question—"What will we do when the people refuse to give?" My answer was, "We will let it die and its glory be embalmed." However, I reminded him that if we taught the Bible to these young people one summer we would have to wait until we got to heaven to know how much good it had done. I also pointed out that Mars Hill Bible School died—but its glory was embalmed, and the preachers trained by T. B. Larimore in that old Bible school led thousands to Christ. I promised the elders that the very year and day that members of this congregation would not sacrifice for this good work we would not raise a little finger to keep its glory from being embalmed. The elders unanimously said to give it a try. We got busy and raised enough money ourselves to buy six tents. We took the special collection and were on our way to Short Mountain.

To our delight and surprise the support of the Bible camp grew and today we own (just 20 minutes up the interstate) a marvelous camp of our own that is beautifully equipped and used each summer for intensive Bible training. Thousands of our young people have been blessed and many have been encouraged to go to Christian colleges. Hundreds and hundreds have been involved in this worthy program of teaching the young. We shudder to think what would have happened if 25 years ago our elders had said: "We are not about to get involved in taking care of a bunch of kids during the summer." If this had been the case, it would have been so tragic, so heartbreaking, so wrong.

"We ain't got no money" should not stop an idea whose time has come, when the program is right and good and the desire behind it strong and worthy.

I want to share one more illustration of doing great things when "we ain't got no money." A few years ago Madison decided that we must get into color television. We simply could not let this new and mysterious media be used by the devil and his crowd and not make an attempt to use it for the glory of God and the spread of the kingdom. To our amazement and surprise we learned that everything about color television was expensive, and at that time we really needed two million dollars to get into it right. Here we were wanting to use television locally and nationally with a network quality program, and yet not a cent in the budget was available for it. But the desire was strong and right and good. One of the television stations, now owned by General Electric, heard of our desire and made us a proposition. They would buy the mobile equipment, use it seven days a week, and lease it to us only on Sunday for the program at a reasonable rate if we would sign a long term contract. This was the break we needed, and yet we still did not have the money. We asked the elders if we could film this program on Sunday evening, and at the close of the program when we were off the air simply say to our members that we were going to pass the basket and ask each one of them who was able and who was willing, to make a special sacrifice and give a little extra in order that we may pay for this program.

Well, these farsighted elders who were in love with the Lord and who wanted his word spread so badly replied that we should give it a try. To our delight the contribution on Sunday night paid for the entire telecast, and has done so now for over eleven years. The program is given to local congregations across the nation, and all they have to do is pay for the time at their local station. Tens of thousands of people have been reached, souls have been converted, and brethren have been edified because of the program. People have heard of the New Testament church, and the good that has come cannot be calculated by mere

129

human beings. When we think of the program being seen in such cities as Chicago, Indianapolis, Detroit, Atlanta and Oklahoma City, as well as one series on the Armed Services Network, we shudder to think what would have happened if these elders had said: "We are not about to launch out on a program of such magnitude."

I hope these three programs will serve as illustrations of what can be done when "we ain't got no money." Of course we must use good judgment, and we must never obligate the church in a way that would bring reproach. We must count the cost, and yet, within the framework of what is right and sound and solid, there are so many programs of work that can be done when we will really make an all out effort.

130

To Him That Hath
It Shall Be Given,
And He Shall Have Abundance

Our blessed Lord gives us a parable in the 25th chapter of the book of Matthew, beginning with verse 14 through verse 30 that we believe teaches lessons that are essential for church growth. We know of no other passage in all the Bible that is more needed by the congregations than this lesson. Please read the parable carefully.

**Activity stimulates activity, and inactivity
stimulates inactivity.**

For the kingdom of heaven is as a man travelling into a far country, who called his own servants, and delivered unto them his goods. And unto one he gave five talents, to another two, and to another one; to every man according to his several ability; and straightway took his journey. Then he that had received the five talents went and traded with the same, and made them other five talents. And likewise he that had received two, he also gained

131

other two. But he that had received one went and digged in the earth, and hid his lord's money. After a long time the lord of those servants cometh, and reckoneth with them. And so he that had received five talents came and brought other five talents, saying, Lord thou deliveredst unto me five talents: behold, I have gained beside them five talents more. His lord said unto him, Well done, thou good and faithful servant: thou hast been faithful over a few things, I will make thee ruler over many things: enter thou into the joy of thy lord. He also that had received two talents came and said, Lord thou deliveredst unto me two talents: behold, I have gained two other talents beside them. His lord said unto him, Well done, good and faithful servant; thou hast been faithful over a few things, I will make thee ruler over many things: enter thou into the joy of thy lord. Then he which had received the one talent came and said, Lord, I knew thee that thou art a hard man, reaping where thou hast not sown, and gathering where thou hast not strawed: And I was afraid, and went and hid thy talent in the earth: lo, there thou hast that is thine. His lord answered and said unto him, Thou wicked and slothful servant, thou knewest that I reap where I sowed not, and gather where I have not strawed: Thou oughtest therefore to have put my money to the exchangers, and then at my coming I should have received mine own with usury. Take therefore the talent from him, and give it unto him which hath ten talents. For unto every one that hath shall be given, and he shall have abundance: but from him that hath not shall be taken away even that which he hath. And cast ye the unprofitable servant into outer darkness: there shall be weeping and gnashing of teeth.

Note that the talents do not represent ability, but opportunity. Not every individual has the same opportunity; not every congregation has the same opportunity. However, every individual and every congregation has some opportunity. The talents were given according to the ability, and therefore represent the opportunity.

I wish every elder, deacon, and Bible school teacher could understand that the worst mistake that can be made is the sin of "donothingness." Note the one talent man did not squander and waste his talent. His problem was that he was fearful and did nothing. Jesus gave him the most scathing denunciation in all of holy writ and told him that he was wicked and slothful and should be bound hand and foot and cast into outer darkness. What did he do to receive such a scathing denunciation from the Master? The answer is nothing, absolutely nothing. Note that the five talent man and the two talent man used their opportunity and God gave them more. Then Jesus states a principle that those of us in leadership in the local church would do well to quote every day of our lives. This principle is true and right, for it comes from the word of God. It is this: "For unto every one that hath shall be given, and he shall have abundance: but from him that hath not shall be taken away even that which he hath."

I have seen this happen with my own eyes over the last half a century and can testify that not only from holy writ, but from actual experience it is true.

Let me illustrate.

A little more than 25 years ago, I knew two congregations that were similar in many respects. They were both located in a great southern city, and each one was blessed with a marvelous location on a multi-million dollar four-lane highway. Each one was cast in a community that was destined to grow and each one had a modest building that was filled to capacity, accommodating comfortably about 350 or 400 people. Now note the contrast.

Congregation *A* took this attitude. "We are out of debt, we have a nice building, we are rolling nicely, let us sit steady in the boat." The devil and the angels of hell could not have made a better speech or fostered an attitude more destined to mark the end of growth.

A few hundred miles away in another southern city, a congregation that we will call Congregation *B* had the same problem. When they met, one of the old gray-headed elders rose and said, in essence, "Brethren, God has given us a great opportunity. We have a location here on this multi-million dollar highway, and the town is growing. The time is right for us to launch out into the deep. Let us remember that we must take advantage of every opportunity, and we must start today to plan big things for God, and to leave enough room in our plans for his providential help. Let us not be afraid for God is with us. Let us set goals, dream dreams, and launch out into the deep." The younger men all agreed, and the congregation in the modest building, without even a building fund made their plans and launched out.

Now 30 years have rolled by, and let us look at the results. Is it really true that "to him that hath it shall be given"? Is it really true when we use what God gives us he gives us more? Is it really true that when we take advantage of one opportunity, that God will open another door, and when we take advantage of that, another and another and another?

Congregation A is still located in the same place. The population of the town has increased, but, alas, the congregation that was once 400 has gone down. They will do well to have 60 in Sunday school and Bible school on any given Sunday. Negativism has taken over, and they have quarreled among themselves. They did not use the opportunity that God gave them, and he took it away. It is a heartbreaking situation.

Now let us note Congregation B. What has happened to these people who used what God gave them and launched out into the deep with enthusiasm and vigor and dedication? The little plant is gone, and there is an auditorium that seats 3,000 and is used four times on Sunday morning. Their record Bible school attendance for one Sunday is 8,400. They have missionaries in many countries. They have taken care of over 1,000 homeless children. Their record cash collection on a Sunday morning is $462,000. The congregation is of one heart, one mind, and one soul. They have never had a split, never had division, never had a fuss, never had a fight. The congregation is blessed by helping the poor, the homeless and the

135

aged, by providing quality education for the children, and by sending missionaries to various parts of the world.

What a contrast between Congregation A and B. And yet the explanation is as simple as ABC, and it is as true and binding a principle as is found anywhere. The answer is Matthew 25:29, "For unto every one that hath shall be given, and he shall have abundance: but from him that hath not shall be taken away even that which he hath."

I believe in the church in Jerusalem, (the model church) and I believe that God intends for every congregation to be active, wide-awake, enthusiastic, and always striving to take advantage of every opportunity. I have seen this attitude in congregations with only a handful of members, and I have seen God bless a church. It is not a matter of size, it is a matter of attitude and principle. Note that the two talent man received the same commendation as the five talent man. He used what he had, he launched out into the deep, and he was blessed.

Activity stimulates activity, and inactivity stimulates inactivity. It is a matter of using what we have or losing it. God opens many doors of opportunity, and it is ours to take advantage of them. The door of the ark stood open, but there came a time when God closed the door and when he did, it was closed forever. Sometimes a great opportunity is given, and when spurned the door is closed forever.

What a thrilling and delightful thing it is to be a part of a church that takes advantage of every opportunity, that launches out into the deep, that really

makes a difference in the community, in the brotherhood, and in the world, that is active, wide awake
and dynamic, and always alert for every opportunity
to do more for him who did so much for us.

The Loss
Of Woman Power

I have already mentioned in this book Stan Lillie, who served the Madison church for many years as an elder. He was one of the most brilliant men I have ever known, and he certainly was one of the most brilliant church leaders I have ever met. One day he said to me: "You know, commissioner, one of the great tragedies of our day is the loss of woman power. You see," he went on to say, "Dupont, where I served as Personnel Manager for all these years, could not survive without its woman power. No political party can elect a candidate without woman power. And yet in the church of our Lord where there is so much to be done, we tell our women, in essence, to sit down on the back seat, be quiet, and do nothing."

And when we meet the real need of real people, we begin to grow.

Brother Lillie went on to explain that he knew there were certain things that a woman was not to do in the New Testament church. For example, she was not to be an elder, because she certainly could not be the husband of one wife. And he pointed out that it never pleased God for women to be pulpit preachers, as is evident in the teaching of Paul and of the New Testament. However, he pointed out that while there were a few restrictions there were hundreds and hundreds of things that women could do, and many of them better than men.

I agreed with Brother Lillie. One area where women are so valuable in the local church is the Sunday school. Most of our teachers at Madison are women. In fact we divide the boys from the girls beginning in about the third grade. This we do so that the older women can teach the younger women and influence their Christian character. We also have in some of the young people's classes a husband and wife team to teach, and this has proven very successful.

It is our custom to have an artist for every department in Sunday school in order that we may have our rooms blazing with enthusiasm and optimism and teaching the word of God. About nine out of ten of the artists we train are women.

Another delightful work is the grading of the World Bible School papers. In the East, the White Bluff congregation in White Bluff, Tennessee, can be contacted and in the West, Jimmie Lovell, 3105 Palos Verdes Drive North, Palos Verdes Estates, California 92074. Many women in the congregation can spend their spare time accepting the responsibility of being a teacher for those who have enrolled across the sea. Both men and women are active in this great work and receive a lot of satisfaction. It is nice to give reports in the bulletin and to share enthusiasm with other members of the congregation. Remember, activity stimulates activity.

Each one of our Sunday school departments has a secretary, and these are mostly women. A dozen or so women work full time at the Madison church, using their professional skills as secretaries to help us advance the cause of Christ.

In the field of benevolence we also depend on women. In fact, probably three-fourths of the work in this area is done by women. We have a different group that sews each evening. They are different ages and interested in making different things for the poor. Thousands of new dresses and garments of every kind have been made by these women.

In our Meals-on-Wheels program about 75 percent of those involved are women.

I have noticed with interest the marvelous work the volunteer ladies do in the local hospital. In many of our hospitals in Nashville, Tennessee, it is unbelievable what a skillful, dedicated, wonderful staff some of these volunteers are making. It is good for the volunteer because it is good to give yourself and your time to a great noble cause.

Why could not the church have a program for its volunteers to assist the poor, to help in teaching the word of God, and to assist in many ways?

For example, we are blessed with several registered nurses in the Madison church. Anita Elliott, one of our elders' wives, heads a program of home service for our sick. She either goes by herself or sends a

141

registered nurse by that home each day to check on this person. The person is generally old or has a problem sufficient enough that someone should check them every day. This nurse is able to take their blood pressure, their temperature, and call the doctor for them to keep him informed, or if they need to go to the doctor a transportation program has been arranged by these volunteer women. Their presence is a great blessing, and not only helps these volunteers but really and truly helps those in need.

I am not trying to give a list of all the programs of work, but I am convinced the need is there. And when we meet the real need of real people, we begin to grow. The church is seen as a relevant, glorious, wonderful institution. However, when we do not use our woman power and do not give our members a chance to give themselves in the cause of Christ, we sometimes cause our young people to wonder, "Is the church really relevant to the twentieth century? Does the church really make a difference in the lives of people? Is it really important when it comes to human beings?" The congregation that involves its woman power gives a clear "yes" to answer those questions.

I wanted to mention another program that for 20 years has been such a great blessing—our visitation by ladies of the church to nursing homes in the community. For about 20 years they have visited each nursing home where they have left a bud vase and take a fresh cut flower to each patient. Some of these older patients have one visit per week, and that is the wonderful lady from the Madison church of Christ who comes by to see them and brings them a flower.

The most wonderful thing about this program is its consistency—day after day, week after week, year after year, every Monday morning at 9 o'clock the ladies go out and the flowers go out.

It has brought comfort and consolation and help to so many in the past 20 years. It really is not the flowers, but the love and the care and the concern that touches so many hearts. We have a different group of ladies for each of the four nursing homes, because we do not want it to be too big a burden on any of these ladies.

Visitation, teaching, and benevolent work all can provide a wonderful service for women in the local church. May God bless them each one.

143

Involvement, A Necessity

We all understand that if we have a talent and do not use it we will lose it. However, it is also true of members of the church. If you do not use them, put them to work in other words, you are much more likely to lose them.

The key is to have a program that is so broad, so deep, and so wonderful that every member can discover his own niche. Not all of us are the same, and we must be careful not to consider our work important and all the other programs unimportant.

A few years ago we converted a prisoner and he came to services. About the same time we also had a very fine couple visit us at services. The man in charge of our personal evangelism sent the ex-prisoner and another man to see them. They did not have much culture or refinement or manners. The young couple was offended and never returned to services. We made a mistake in sending the wrong couple to visit those young people. There were many things in the church program that these two could have done that would have resulted in good.

A few years ago I thanked a group of men who were carpenters and plumbers for helping us build our cabins at the Bible camp. To my surprise they thanked us and said, "You don't know how wonderful it is to be able to use our skill and our talent for the glory of God and for the good of mankind. We really feel like we are making a contribution."

The key is to have a program that is so broad, so deep, and so wonderful that every member can discover his own niche.

It was my privilege some time ago to help dedicate the new building at Highland Oaks in Dallas, Texas. We had 7,100 in Bible school (a record for churches of Christ in Texas). We were so delighted to see lawyers, doctors, engineers, dentists, and business men working like beavers. Many of them were parking cars. Others were in the tent putting up tables and arranging food. There were many, many details to be looked after on that day, for to handle a crowd of this size with smoothness requires a lot of planning, a lot of cooperation, and a lot of help. Some of the men had walkie talkies and were able to park the crowd and enjoy a beautiful day.

This spirit of being willing to cooperate and to perform a menial task is essential to church growth. Jesus taught us in the great lesson in John 13:4-9, that we are to wash each others' feet. Members of the church who think they are too good, or too big, or too im-

146

portant to roll up their sleeves and pitch in and become involved in a great and good work are most unfortunate.

One quickly senses in a congregation where the members are not involved in something other than holding services.

Of course we want members to attend services, but this alone is not enough. I am convinced that legalism and Phariseeism, so condemned by our blessed Lord, is not nearly as likely to happen in our day and time if we are involved. But, if all we do is attend the worship, never becoming involved in visitation, benevolent work, mission work or other great programs of the church, it is easy for us to look down our nose and say, "Lord, I am so thankful I'm not as others are, and Lord, I do this and I do that." However, when you are involved in a program of church work, and are really helping the poor and the lowly and the downtrodden, teaching the word of God, sending missionaries, visitation, etc., you want to smite your breast and say, "Oh Lord, be merciful to me, a sinner."

One of the great challenges of leadership in our day is to inaugurate a program of work in the local church that is so broad, so deep, so important, and so wonderful that every single member of the congregation can become involved and be a part of it.

Visitation

I enjoy telling the story of a conversation I had a few years ago with Campbell Jenkins, president of Tennessee Real Estate Company. Mr. Jenkins had experienced tremendous success in the real estate business, and as a young man, I was asking him to share his secret with me. He first assured me that there were really only three rules in buying real estate that one had to keep in mind in order to succeed. Immediately I reached for my fountain pen and prepared to write down these three golden rules that would carry me to success in all real estate transactions.

I am convinced that there are at least three rules for a growing Sunday morning Bible school.

"Now the first rule in succeeding in real estate," Mr. Jenkins said, "is location." He then went into great detail to explain that it is not what the land is but where it is that makes it valuable. He pointed to a piece of property on a four-lane intersection that was sold by the foot at a tremendous price, and pointed out the same amount of land could be bought in my hometown for very little, but then he explained the difference was location. Ninety thousand people per day passed this corner, and maybe nine people per day would pass the corner of the land I mentioned in my home county.

Now being young and impetuous, I was anxious to get on to the next point. And so I said immediately, "All right, I have the first point down. Now please give me the second rule." He asked me if I was sure I was ready, and I assured him I was. Then he said, "The second rule is location." Immediately I replied, "Let me guess the third rule is location." And he said, "You're right. Now you have all three. If you have a piece of property and the location is right, then brother you have an investment."

I have never forgotten this bit of homespun advice from a distinguished business man. I think of his advice often when it comes to the word visitation. In building a congregation and a Bible school, there is one area in which it is almost impossible to fail—and that area is visitation.

Several years ago we read of a congregation that enjoyed one hundred in Bible school, but they met and made a vow that for three years they would visit on Monday night every newcomer, every visitor, and every absentee in their Sunday morning Bible school. The growth was phenomenal.

Jesus had something to say about visitation in the 25th chapter of Matthew, verses 41-45.

Then shall he say also unto them on the left hand, Depart from me, ye cursed, into everlasting fire, prepared for the devil and his angels: For I was an hungered, and ye gave me no meat: I was thirsty, and ye gave me no drink: I was a stranger, and ye took me not in: naked, and ye clothed me not: sick, and in prison, and ye visited me not. Then shall they also answer him, saying, Lord, when saw we thee an hungered, or athirst, or a stranger, or naked, or sick, or in prison, and did not minister unto thee? Then shall he answer them, saying, Verily I say unto you, Inasmuch as ye did it not to one of the least of these, ye did it not to me.

There is, I believe, a therapeutic value in visitation. When you get out into the real world where the babies are being born and people are dying, and you visit, you are indeed in the real world. I have learned over the years that if we become a little blue and despondent the best antidote is visitation. Why don't you try it sometime? Get up and visit the shut-ins, the hospital patients, the old people.

The late Stan Lillie, that we have mentioned often in this book, was a master at visitation. He visited every single family and was very alert to any new families. One day a lady told us this interesting story. She had just moved to Madison and needed to go to the store for a moment. She left her children and walked around the corner to the neighborhood grocery store. When she came back she saw a strange gray-haired man standing at the door. He opened the door for her and said: "It's all right, Mary, it's just old Brother Lillie from the church of Christ. I came to welcome you to town and see if there is anything that you or the children need, or if there is anything we can do for you."

Such visitation endeared him to the entire church.

We need to encourage visitation in every department and on every level. We need to visit the newcomers. We need to visit those who are new converts. We need to visit those who are absent from Sunday school. We need to visit those in our own subdivision or street who are members of the church.

In our day and age there are some obstacles to visiting. Night time visiting is not safe by oneself in certain sections of the big city. And yet visitation still has its power.

Many congregations divide up into small units and look after each other by means of a visitation program that is well organized. We have 166 neighborhood groups here at Madison, and each group has a leader. We ask them to be responsible for the few families that live close to them, and report any illness, or deaths, or anything that comes along in which we can be of service.

I am convinced that there are at least three rules for a growing Sunday morning Bible school. (1) Visitation, (2) Visitation, (3) Visitation. Let us go back to the old fashioned way of visiting each other.

Let Us Remember What Is Required

God does not require that we be big, or wealthy, or powerful, or super smart. What our Heavenly Father requires is faithfulness. The important thing and the absolutely essential thing is for us to be faithful. The apostle Paul teaches us that faithfulness is ours to plant and water and cultivate, but it is God's to give the increase. Let us not be too interested in numbers or bigness, but let us be vitally interested in faithfulness.

I do believe that if we are faithful, God will bless us, and the way to build a growing church is to be faithful. Our success must be measured in terms of faithfulness. We must never lose sight of the value and preciousness of the individual. It has been my experience that congregations that have begun to reach anywhere near the peak of their potential, have been congregations where the emphasis is on the individual.

153

It is good to be goal oriented, and it is good to strive to do better every day in every program. I am often asked how many do you want in Bible school?

The answer is simply one more.

Jesus said leave the 99 and go after the one. When we are willing to knock every door in the community, swim the mighty river, and climb the mountain in order to reach one more little boy or girl for Christ, then we have the spirit that is going to lead us into acceptable growth. Part of the balance for which we plead in this book, and part of the balance of the model church in Jerusalem was the interest in the individual, the value of the soul, the worth of each soul, and the importance of each one being faithful. "Be thou faithful unto death, and I will give thee a crown of life" (Revelation 2:10).

Let us not be too interested in numbers or bigness, but let us be vitally interested in faithfulness.

May we hear the Father say at that last great day, "Well done, good and faithful servant. You have been faithful over a few things, and I will make thee ruler over many."

Amen